Is
Christianity
true?

by

John Benton

EVANGELICAL PRESS
12 Wooler Street, Darlington, Co. Durham, DL1 1RQ,
England.

First published 1988

ISBN 0-85234-260-8

Typeset by Outset Graphics, Hartlepool.
Printed in Great Britain by Cox and Wyman, Reading.

To Matthew, Tom, Jessica and Owen.
The unsearchable riches of Christ are
the best treasure and the greatest
inheritance I can give you.
With all my love, Daddy.

'If there is an angel who records the sorrows of men as well as their sins, he knows how many and deep are the sorrows that spring from false ideas for which no man is culpable.'

George Eliot, *Silas Marner*

'Knowledge cannot save us, but we cannot be saved without knowledge. Faith is not on this side of knowledge but beyond it. We must necessarily come to knowledge first, though we must not stay at it when we are come thither.'

John Donne, *Christmas Day Sermon 1621*

Contents

Acknowledgements

I would like to extend my thanks
–   To Ranald Macauley of the L'Abri Fellowship, Switzerland, for allowing me to use some material from his lecture, 'How we know that Christianity is true', given in Guildford in 1984, on the moral argument for God.
–   To John Horrocks and Jeni Croft for reading through the manuscript and making a number of helpful suggestions and improvements.
–   To Jen Watkins for turning my hieroglyphics into a readable manuscript.
–   Above all to my wife Ann, who has loved me and been a blessing to me through all the difficult days which seem to have accompanied the birth of this book.

John Benton

Introduction –
The king's new clothes

The children's story of the king's suit of clothes is very well known and was popularized in a song, many years ago now, by the American entertainer Danny Kaye. The story goes something like this. There is a very foolish, proud and vain king who relishes being in the height of fashion and who very much enjoys feeling himself to be the object of other people's admiration. To his court come two swindlers who pretend to be able to sell him the most elegant and beautiful suit of clothes which has ever been tailored.

Actually they have nothing at all. But their trickery is to play upon the king's vanity by telling him that to a foolish person the suit is invisible. Only wise people can see it. The wise alone can see and recognize it as the most wonderful set of clothing. The swindlers open their wares, and the king, wishing to appear wise and not a fool, pretends, 'Ah yes, of course. What marvellous garments!' He asks his courtiers what they think and they too, not wishing to appear fools, enthusiastically concur that this is the most wonderful suit of clothes they have ever seen, 'just the thing for the coming public parade!' (One wonders if there isn't some wicked humour in their suggesting this as they play along with their vain king!)

At the parade the people too, having heard the story and keen to be known as wise citizens, give their loud approval of the king's clothes. Only one small boy, who has no idea what is going on and who does not understand the ways and motivations of adults, is shocked beyond measure. 'Look at the king!' he shouts, and to everyone's consternation he blurts out the fact that the king is naked! By this time, of course, the swindlers have departed with their money.

There are two elements in this story which work for the success of the trick. The first is the nature of the swindlers' claim. The suit is not an object open to common enquiry because to anyone who says that he cannot see the suit, the swindlers' answer is simply, 'Well, that is because you are not wise enough.' Thus *their claim* concerning the suit *is not open to ordinary methods of proof*. In the last analysis it is completely unverifiable; there is no way of knowing whether or not they are telling the truth if you are not one of the 'wise'. So it is very subtle. The claim that the suit is only visible to the wise panders to people's love of élitism (oh, to be one of a select few!), and yet avoids the burden of being open to the common methods of proof and enquiry.

Secondly, what helps the trick is *the force of human concern about 'what other people think of me'*. That common human characteristic works in the swindlers' favour. The king doesn't wish to appear foolish to the swindlers; the courtiers do not wish to appear foolish to the king. Because people are so very concerned not to appear foolish in front of their friends and peers they will even pretend to something that is not true. How many of us have made exaggerated claims in order to impress our friends at different times! So the trick proceeds.

Now this brings us to the point of this book. Some people say that religion is, at root, this kind of confidence trick. They would say that the substance of religion is subjective and personal, it is about personal prayer and conscience and religious feelings, and therefore not open to common enquiry. God is only real to the faithful. And for those who don't have faith and may have the temerity to question things, these critics would say the stock answer is 'Well, God doesn't seem real to you because you haven't got enough faith.' God is therefore just like the king's suit of clothes: he is not open to ordinary enquiry.

Then, the criticism would go on to say, once people have been lured into making some initial religious commitment, they are kept to it by 'what other people will think of me'. They do not wish to be seen by their friends to have made a foolish move, a decision which they now perhaps regret, so they stick it out with their religion. They continue to bluff it out, perhaps even trying to fool themselves.

We have to say that this is a very reasonable theory and its description of religion and religious belief may be entirely accurate in some circumstances. However, the purpose of this book is to try to show that it is not possible to put Bible Christianity into that category. The aim is to set out some straightforward reasons for believing that Christianity is actually true.

We shall see that not only does Christianity claim to be the truth, but also it deliberately invites and encourages open enquiry. It invites investigation and discussion. It feels it has nothing to lose by honest questioning, and indeed everything to gain. Christianity claims that the evidence for it is strong. It encourages people to use their minds. It is contended that Christianity is far from being a leap in the dark, which, once made, is secured by a fear of losing face in the eyes of others. Rather it is eminently reasonable in the light of the evidence.

The Christian does not claim he can prove *everything* he believes. Though in another way perhaps he can, as we shall see later. But although faith is not the same as sight, the Christian does claim he can prove *enough to make faith reasonable and even inevitable*. Christianity does involve faith, but unlike the story of the king's suit of clothes it is not wishful thinking or blind faith. Becoming a Christian means taking a step of faith. But it is a step of faith firmly based upon facts. It is a step which proceeds logically from those facts. This book seeks to set out something of the factual basis for Christianity. It seeks, with God's help, to lead you, the reader, to faith in Christ.

1.
Nothing more than feelings?

The car radio was on as I drove through the early morning traffic into London. In the middle of the record programme came the usual religious slot. *Thought for the Day* that morning was a moving meditation from Psalm 14 on the existence and reality of God. The speaker finished and his background music died away. The programme went straight into the next record, a popular song beginning with the words, 'Feelings . . . nothing more than feelings . . .'

Whether that was just a coincidence or whether the choice of that particular record was meant to be a subtle comment by the programme's producer on what had just gone before, I do not know. But it seemed to sum up the attitude of so many people towards religion and towards Christianity: 'God? . . . Church? . . . It's just feelings . . . nothing more than feelings.'

The popular idea prevails that Christian faith is nothing more than a vague mixture of sentimentality and wishful thinking. It is unreal. Christian conversion is dismissed as 'just psychological' and it is accepted without question that it does not really involve actual contact with a living God.

Very often people assume this to be the case without giving the matter much thought. The ethos and assumptions of the society in which we live exert a powerful influence upon us. This generally accepted assumption can prejudice us against ever seriously considering Christianity.

Can religion and Christianity be dismissed so easily? Are Christians just gullible people who have never thought these things through? What does Christianity have to say in reply to this kind of critique?

The idea that faith is 'nothing more than feelings' can take two forms. Here is the first one.

1. 'Christian faith is an unreal solution to manufactured needs.'

Advertising seems to meet us everywhere we go these days. We are frustrated people, never quite fulfilling our vast potential, but if only we buy this new deodorant . . . if only we buy this new car . . . if only we invest in this new unit trust . . . then all the barriers which hinder us being the great people we could be will disappear and we will blossom into a new quality of life! Or so the impression is given. A large part of the advertising industry spends its time seeking to persuade us that certain products, which we *can* live without, are essential to us. The TV, the magazines, the hoardings, can be used to make us feel that we desperately need things which in fact we do not. They can manufacture needs in us. They plant the need in us and then sell us the product. Is this the same game which religion plays?

The church or the evangelist wants to gain a following, so they work on us to make us feel that we need what they have to offer. Faith fulfils a manufactured need. It was never a real need. It was planted in us by the preacher. We can do without it. Conversions are purely the result of clever crowd psychology and manipulation. That is what some would say.

Around the turn of the century the Russian physiologist Ivan Pavlov achieved world renown by his researches into the formation of conditioned reflexes in dogs. Through electrical shock treatment he stimulated the dogs into a state of physical and emotional collapse. He found that while they were in this condition it was relatively easy to introduce fresh activities into their pattern of behaviour. It was possible to make the poor dogs do what he wanted them to do.

Transferring such methods to human beings has produced brainwashing techniques used by various governments and certain extreme religious cults to indoctrinate people into their way of thinking. Now, on a smaller, more subtle scale perhaps, is this what Christianity is about?[1]

In responding to such a charge, the Christian would want to say basically three things.

Firstly, *the Christian would not wish to deny the possibility of psychological manipulation; indeed he would want to warn against it.* For example, John White was until recently Professor of Psychiatry at the University of Manitoba in Canada and is also a committed Christian. He warns us about such techniques in religious meetings in one of his books.[2] He points out that the recipe used in such meetings is as follows:

1.   People are softened up and made a little anxious by the speaker frequently switching between talking in first a loud and then a soft voice.

2.   Then folk are made to feel very guilty as the impression is given that not only God, but the speaker himself, knows all about their secret sins.

3.   The next step is to try to destroy people's judgement by continually changing the emotional tone of the meeting. Perhaps a very weepy story is told, then the speaker might appear to become very angry, but then this is followed by a joke, and so on. This disorientates people's thinking.

4.   Then the same cliché is repeated fairly rhythmically over and over again describing what the speaker wants people to do.

5. Finally, if the meeting can be set up so that it takes place at a time when the listeners are physically tired, or such that there is a lot of emotional music, then the chances of getting people to make some kind of religious decision are even greater.

In this way it is only too possible to get lots of 'converts'. But of course it is all unreal and such methods must be rejected and condemned as an attack on the dignity of human beings.

Secondly, *Christianity would want us to note the whole aim of such methods.* The aim of the psyched-up emotion and the manipulative techniques is to disorientate people so that they temporarily lose the power to judge things properly. The aim is to knock out the mind. It can be argued that this is even the case to a lesser extent with certain forms of advertising. Once people are no longer thinking for themselves, they can be swept along on a wave of emotion, and they are open to be pressurized into a manufactured religious decision. When the mind is bypassed the dangers are obvious.

But, thirdly, having noticed the aims of such techniques, it is very interesting and illuminating to look at the Bible, the sourcebook of Christianity. Here we find that the Bible stridently distances itself from all such methods. Instead of telling people to leave their minds at home when they come to church, by contrast it emphasizes that we must use our minds. We must use them not only in our everyday lives but also in our approach to God. This is plain for at least five reasons.

1. According to the Bible God is the Creator and he created human beings with the powers of thought and reason. The God who gave us these gifts wants us to use them. To devalue the place of the mind is to despise what God has given.

2. The Christian gospel, God's good news for the world, is a message addressed to our minds. God does not bring people into his kingdom by zapping them with

some strange religious experience which they cannot explain and which bypasses their thought processes. Because people come to God through a message, the Bible asks the questions: 'How, then, can they call on the one they have not believed in? And how can they believe in the one of whom they have not heard? And how can they hear without someone preaching to them?' It concludes, 'Consequently, faith comes by hearing the message, and the message is heard through the word of Christ' (Romans 10:14,17).

3.   The men who wrote the Gospels recording the life and work of Jesus again urge us in the direction of careful thought concerning Christianity. This is how Luke, the writer of the third Gospel, begins his book: 'Many have undertaken to draw up an account of the things that have been fulfilled among us, just as they were handed down to us by those who from the first were eyewitnesses and servants of the word. Therefore, since I myself have carefully investigated everything from the beginning, it seemed good also to me to write an orderly account for you, most excellent Theophilus, so that you may know the certainty of the things you have been taught' (Luke 1:1-4). Luke stresses to his friend Theophilus the importance of research into the facts and the use of the mind.

4.   The Bible does not exclude the possibility of ecstatic religious experience but is very careful about it. Rather, the Holy Spirit, in whom God meets directly with people, is described as One who brings the fruit of self-control and of a sound mind (Galatians 5:23; 2 Timothy 1:7).

5.   The immense importance of the mind is also seen in the nature of the New Testament evangelism. For example in Ephesus, as the apostle Paul sought to bring the gospel to that city, he hired a lecture hall and every day for two years he taught and listened and answered people's questions there. One of the early manuscripts

of the New Testament* has a margin note that this went
on for about five hours each day. If that is true, it means
something like 3000 hours of lecturing and discussion.
That involves more mental activity than many university
courses today! In Athens Paul went to the Areopagus,
where the philosophers of the day gathered, and he
argued the case for Christianity with them. There is no
bypassing of the mind in New Testament evangelism.
Rather Paul addresses people's minds, he wants them to
use their minds, indeed he stretches their minds.

It would be wrong to give the impression that the
Bible is saying that the mind is the only thing that matters. There is a great place for the emotions, and indeed
for every aspect of human personality in Christian faith.
But we must conclude that the Christianity of the Bible
will have nothing to do with mindless religion, and nor
should we.

That being the case, to try to explain away Christianity as an unreal solution to psyched-up problems
really does not fit the facts. It attacks a straw man. It
does not dispose of Christianity.

Nothing more than feelings? A second approach
which seeks to dismiss Christianity as being thoughtless
emotionalism can be summarized in the following way.

2. 'Christian faith is an unreal solution to real human needs.'

This is the old familiar taunt that Christianity is just a
crutch for the weak. The realities of life are hard. Needs
are real and religion is nothing but a comforting
escapism. As people who cannot face life might, sadly,
turn to drink or to taking a drug to help them feel better,
so people take religion. It solves none of the problems
but it is a soothing fantasy. Thus the atheist Karl Marx
dismissed religion in his famous phrase as the 'opiate of
the people'. The lot of the poor in this world is dreadfully
hard, so they comfort themselves in their misery with

false wishful thinking about a happy life beyond the grave.

Marx went on to attack religion further because he felt that this 'opium' served only to stupefy people into inaction concerning the hard circumstances in which they live. It serves to smother the needed revolution. He spoke of religion as 'the flowers on the chains of our oppression'.

Apart from Karl Marx, other influential figures of the last century, such as the philosopher Feuerbach and the father of modern psychiatry, Sigmund Freud, have taken a similar line. God did not create man, they say, but rather man has created God. God is a comforting illusion. Having outgrown the security of home and parents we project a father-figure onto the cosmos in order to help us cope with the frightening helplessness of being alone and inadequate in a barren hostile universe subject to the inexorable laws of nature. Faith in God is thus explained away.

At first sight this approach, adopted by such giants of modern thought, seems to be a very powerful argument against religion. But in fact it is something of a paper tiger as a case against God. Let us note at least four criticisms which can be made of it.

1.   To begin with it is not a very solid argument because it deals with the subject very much at the level of caricature. It pictures all religious people as emotional weaklings who cannot stand on their own feet. It believes the TV comedy image of the effeminate cleric and labels all Christians as spineless. This might do for the slapstick knock-about logic of the political hustings but not for serious thought. It is a foolish assumption to say that before their conversion all Christians were weaklings. Some Christians may have been and may still be emotional weaklings, but for this argument to hold water they must *all* be. And that is quite simply not true by observation.

2.   It is not a very successful argument from the point of view of the opponents of Christianity, because the same argument, if we accept it, can be reversed and used just as well to 'explain away' atheism. We could say with equal logic that Karl Marx, for example, was an atheist firstly, because he was a very strong-willed personality who did not want to think himself answerable to an almighty God, and secondly, because he had been disillusioned by his hypocritical parents who once changed their religion just for the benefit of his father's business prospects. We could say then that such people as Marx 'invent' atheism for their own 'comfort'. If religious belief is simply a function of personality then that can include atheism too!

3.   It is a logically defective argument because it confuses the possible motives as to why someone has become a Christian with the objective question of whether or not God exists and Christianity is true. Where would Agatha Christie be if we all followed such logic as this? Where would the writer of the 'whodunnit' be if we immediately assumed *de facto* that anyone who had a motive *must* have committed the crime? Whether or not mankind has a reason for wanting there to be a God is a completely separate question from whether or not God is actually there. We must not confuse motives with objective truth.

4.   Lastly, such an explanation of Christianity can only stand so long as we view Christianity as a purely subjective matter limited to private prayer, Bible reading, religious experience etc. But that is the very thing which the faith of the Bible will not allow.

Writers of the Old Testament were well aware of the possibility of 'gods' which are only the product of human imagination, but rejected this as a totally inadequate explanation for the God of Israel (e.g. Psalm 115:2-9; Isaiah 40:15-26).

The reality of Israel's God, in contrast with the 'gods'

of the surrounding nations of ancient times, is indicated in a very interesting way by their different type of hymnology and praise. The German scholar Klaus Westermann, in his book *The Praise of God in the Psalms,* describes the distinctiveness of the Israelite hymnody as we find it in the Psalms of the Old Testament. He contrasts it with the other songs to which we have access from other ancient Near-Eastern countries like Egypt and Babylonia addressed to their gods. Westermann distinguishes two kinds of praise, which he calls 'declarative' and 'descriptive' praise. Descriptive praise is praise which praises a god for being so great in what he is, and there is plenty of this in the heathen hymns, thanking the god for being such a great character. As a matter of fact, according to the American scholar Dr Edmund Clowney, there is an element in polytheism that tends to increase this type of praise. In a pantheon of gods there is a necessity to 'butter up' the particular god you are worshipping, in order to make him feel that you are devoted to him more than to other gods, hence feeding the god's pride so that he will listen to you. But one thing that you do not find, which is almost entirely absent from the heathen hymns, compared with those of Israel, is declarative praise. The psalms of Israel are full of declarative praise, that is, *praising God* not simply for what he is, but *for what he has done.* Declarative praise declares the mighty acts of God in delivering his people and providing for their needs. The point is that only a God who is real can act and repeatedly deliver his people. This great difference between the hymnologies of the ancient peoples appears to argue that Israel's God was different from the rest. Israel's God was real. He acted in history.

The New Testament unashamedly demands to be judged in terms of its objective claims. It is a faith rooted in history. It directs us to certain times and certain geographical locations and to certain events which it claims took place there. It points us to objective evidence concerning these things – evidence which is open to scrutiny by anyone. A statement of the apostle Paul concerning the resurrection of Jesus captures the attitude of New Testament Christianity: 'For what I received I passed on to you as of first importance: that Christ died for our sins according to the Scriptures, that he was buried, that he was raised on the third day according to the Scriptures, and that he appeared to Peter, and then to the Twelve. After that, he appeared to more than five hundred of the brothers at the same time, most of whom are still living, though some have fallen asleep. Then he appeared to James, then to all the apostles, and last of all he appeared to me also . . .' (1 Corinthians 15:3-8). Paul refuses to base his belief in the resurrection upon a vague inner religious feeling. He directs his readers to researchable evidence, to eye-witnesses who can be questioned. He argues in the realm of the objective rather than the subjective.

Christians insist that Christianity stands or falls on the veracity of objective matters such as the life, death and resurrection of Jesus. An argument therefore which sees religion as a self-induced illusion rather misses the point when it comes to Christianity. Paul was prepared to put Christianity on the line and say, 'If Christ has not been raised, then our faith is futile' (1 Corinthians 15:17).

This was the approach in the evangelism of the early church. People were not asked to believe primarily in order to solve their personal problems and fears by coming to God. People were not even called first and foremost to believe in Christ that their sins might be forgiven, although that is an immensely important issue. The New Testament evangelists called upon people to believe the gospel primarily because it is *true*. The life, death and resurrection of Jesus had actually occurred, and to ignore it is to live a lie. They called people to become Christians because Christianity is the fact of the matter.

Sometimes today polite people courteously fend off Christianity by saying something like, 'Christianity may be true for you but not for me.' By this they mean, 'Christianity may meet your inner needs but not mine. Christianity may suit your personality and what you are looking for in life but it does not suit me. You may like the Christian faith but it does not appeal to me.' But again, with respect, this totally misses the point. The question is not first of all whether I like Christianity but whether it is the truth. If it is the truth then I have to do something about it. Christianity cannot be relegated to a matter of taste. So the grand question is, 'Is Christianity true?'

*The Western Text: 'from the fifth to the tenth hour' (see R. P. Martin, *Worship in the Early Church,* Eerdmanns, p. 68).

References

1. D.M. Lloyd-Jones, *Conversions Psychological and Spiritual*, IVP, 1959.
2. John White, *The Golden Cow*, Marshall, Morgan & Scott, 1979.

2.
In the beginning, God

The first chapter attempted to answer some objections in order to clear the ground for a consideration of Christianity. Of course, the answering of certain objections to the Christian faith does not itself prove the truth of Christianity's claims. Therefore we must proceed to look at the positive case for Christianity.

Christianity is about God. The Apostles' Creed begins, 'I believe in God the Father Almighty, maker of heaven and earth . . .' The existence of God is obviously central to Christian faith. But is it true? Is God there? Is he real?

Firstly it is essential that we define what we are talking about. A Marplan poll, just before the instalment of Robert Runcie as Archbishop of Canterbury in 1980, asked the question: 'Do you believe in God?' A staggering 73% of all adults questioned answered 'Yes'. That seems a large number for our secular twentieth century. But, of course, the reason for this high percentage of 'yeses' is that the word 'God' was left totally undefined. Thus the question could mean anything people wanted it to mean, so it was not surprising that so many people answered in the affirmative.

Christianity has always asserted that God is. Christianity claims that this God is the only God, the God who has revealed himself in Jesus Christ and who has disclosed his character and ways in the Bible. We must ask, 'Is that reasonable? Does that make sense?' In order to answer that question and in order to avoid the kind of misunderstandings implicit in the Marplan survey, we need first to gather together some of the fundamental things which the Bible says about God, so that we know what we are talking about.

1. The Creator but separate from the creation

Pantheism is the idea that God is everything and everything is God. It equates God with the universe. In his autobiography Bertrand Russell writes of an episode in his early days at Cambridge: 'Having been reading pantheism, I announced to my friends that I was God. They placed candles on each side of me and proceeded to acts of mock worship.'[1]

For reasons which will become apparent later, the Bible flatly contradicts this idea that God is everything. God is the Creator of the world. But there is a definite distinction between God the Creator and his creation. The Bible states that people are wrong to worship the creature rather than the Creator (Romans 1:25). God is other than ourselves and other than his creation. He is intimately involved with the world, but he has a separate existence.

2. The personality of God

The doctrines of the Christian faith speak of God as infinite, eternal and unchangeable. When we hear that kind of language it is easy for us to start thinking of God in terms of some universal force, or colourless impersonal ground of being, the foundation of all that exists. But again the Bible says 'No'. He is infinite, eternal and unchangeable. He is the foundation of all that exists. But he is also *personal*.

Scripture speaks of man being originally made in the image of God. Man has personality and we are not to think of God as being any less than we are. The apostle Paul argues against idolatry in just this way as he is speaking to the Greek thinkers at the Areopagus, the place of debate in ancient Athens. He says, 'Some of your own poets have said, "We are his [God's] off-spring." Therefore since we are God's offspring we should not think that the divine being is like gold or silver or stone' (Acts 17:28,29). Following Paul's line of thought we should conclude, if man is personal and man is less than God, then God must be personal. In fact God is not only personal but goes beyond our ordinary concept of personality. The Scriptures teach the mystery of the Trinity, one God in three persons, Father, Son and Holy Spirit, yet not three gods but one God. Far from his being less than personal, there is, as it were, a super-abundance of personality in God. There are obviously depths here which go beyond our understanding, as we would expect since we are only finite beings and he is the infinite God who made us. In some sense God may be thought of as being suprapersonal, but he is certainly personal and not less than that.

So the Bible speaks of God as having all the attributes of personality. God thinks (Psalm 40:5). He loves (Romans 8:39). He has a will and makes choices (Ephesians 1:9). He communicates (Isaiah 43:1). Note how the psalmist uses similar logic to Paul about the Creator, in his rhetorical questions: 'Does he who implanted the ear not hear? Does he who formed the eye not see? . . . Does he who teaches man lack knowledge?' (Psalm 94:9,10).

3. God is self-sustaining and is the fountain of all other life

When we ask what the precise relationship is between God and the world, it is not possible to give a complete answer. If we could do that we would be God. But we are able to make some things clear

God is the *Creator*. He is the origin of all other existence. The psalmist says of God, 'For with you is the fountain of life; in your light we see light' (Psalm 36:9). In the New Testament Paul writes, 'For from him and through him and to him are all things' (Romans 11:36).

Creation was not a rearrangement of pre-existent matter. Creation by God was *ex nihilo,* out of nothing. 'By faith we understand that the universe was formed at God's command, so that what is seen was not made out of what was visible' (Hebrews 11:3). In fact, again and again throughout the Bible story, this bringing life out of emptiness and barrenness is God's signature. Abraham, the father of the Jewish people, was a very old man and his wife past the age of child-bearing, but God made him the father of many nations (Genesis 17:15-16). Throughout the Old and New Testaments there is the recurring theme of the barren woman being blessed with children: one thinks of the births of Isaac, Jacob and Esau, Samson, Samuel, John the Baptist. This motif, of course, culminates in the miracle of the virgin birth of Christ.

We see the same theme illustrated in the resurrection of Christ. Life is given, by the touch of God, where there had been nothing but death. He is 'God who gives life to the dead and calls things that are not as though they were' (Romans 4:17). All this may seem very strange to us who operate within a universe of seemingly inflexible scientific law. But it should not surprise us that if there is a God who originally set up the universe, and set up its physical laws, he is able to operate outside and above those physical laws to which we are so accustomed.

However, it is not simply in the things which we would term 'miraculous' that God is at work. He upholds and sustains the existence of all things at all times. Nature is a continuous miracle. Paul, in his same speech at Athens says, ' He himself gives all men life and

breath and everything else' (Acts 17:25). The verb is the
present continuous tense. Again he is happy to quote
another Greek poet, saying, 'For in him [God] we live
and move and have our being' (Acts 17:28). Here the
world is represented as totally dependent upon God's
sustaining activity and power every moment of every
day.

By complete contrast, God is dependent upon no
one. God's existence is represented as completely independent and self-sustaining. Jesus said, 'The Father has
life in himself' (John 5:26). Paul again says at Athens,
'He is not served by human hands, as if he needed anything' (Acts 17:25). Paul can write of God 'who alone is
immortal' (1 Timothy 6:16). Technically we speak of the
aseity of God, meaning his independent and underived
existence.

So here is God, having life in himself, independent of
all else, and here is the world totally dependent upon
God, a derived existence. God is the fountain and source
of all that has existence, both as to its origin and its con-
tinuance. In particular man is the creature, God is the
Creator.

4. The holiness of God

God's holiness can refer to his distinctiveness from creation, his 'otherness'. But more specifically it refers to
his perfect moral character. That moral perfection of
God has been disclosed to mankind, for example, in
human conscience and the Ten Commandments, but is
most clearly seen in the life of the Lord Jesus Christ.

God hates all evil and injustice. He has complete and
burning moral integrity. God is light in which there is no
darkness at all, and it is that blazing holiness which,
according to the Bible, leaves the most lasting and

devastating impression upon human beings who come into direct contact with God.

Isaiah's vision of God is an example. 'I saw the Lord seated on a throne, high and exalted, and the train of his robe filled the temple. Above him were seraphs, each with six wings: With two wings they covered their faces', with two they covered their feet, and with two they were flying. And they were calling to one another: "Holy, holy, holy, is the Lord Almighty: the whole earth is full of his glory." At the sound of their voices the doorposts and thresholds shook and the temple was filled with smoke' (Isaiah 6:1-4). Then Isaiah, a good and upright human being, records his reaction to what he saw: '"Woe to me!" I cried, "I am ruined!" For I am a man of unclean lips, and I live among a people of unclean lips, and my eyes have seen the King, the Lord Almighty"' (Isaiah 6:5).

When Job, who in God's own estimation was the most upright man of his day on earth, met with God, this was his overwhelmed response: 'My ears had heard of you but now my eyes see you. Therefore I despise myself and repent in dust and ashes' (Job 42:5,6).

Similar experiences in the lives of the apostles Peter, Paul and John can be found in the New Testament. The most prominent feature which stayed in the minds of these men was of God's burning moral integrity, his shining all-consuming holiness. When a man or a woman has truly met with the living God, says the Bible, there is a reverence which is uncontrived and unselfconscious.

5. The love of God

Yet the Scriptures do not leave us with the impression that God is pure in a clinical and cold way. The life of the Lord Jesus Christ, which ordinary people found so attractive, bears witness to that. God's holiness goes hand in hand with God's love. 'God is love' writes the apostle John (1 John 4:8,16). God did not need creation in order to love. God is love in his being. There is a vibrant torrent of love ever flowing between the persons of the Trinity, and that love overflows to mankind. 'As the Father has loved me, so have I loved you', said Jesus to his disciples (John 15:5).

Love is an idea which is easily misunderstood. The word which especially shows the love of God in the New Testament writings is the Greek word *agape*. This word had little significant pre-Christian usage. It came to the New Testament writers very much as an unused, empty word, into which they poured the fulness of the meaning of the love of God. *Agape* includes friendship and family affection but overflows far beyond their limits. It does not depend on the attractiveness or loveliness of its object and at last comes to encompass even the unlovely enemy (Matthew 5:44). Above all this, it is sacrificial love. It is a love which confers not just limited blessing, but unbounded good upon its object. It is love which spares no costs. Jesus said, 'Greater love has no one than this, that he lay down his life for his friends' (John 15:13). Earlier in his Gospel John tells us, 'For God so loved the world that he gave his one and only Son, that whoever believes in him shall not perish but have eternal life' (John 3:16).

6. The sovereignty of God

The Bible also emphasizes that God is the King, and he is the King in the most absolute sense. He is all-powerful and answerable to no one but himself and his own holy character. God has planned and is now executing all that comes to pass – not in a way which makes void our individual responsibility, accountability and choices; neither is he in any way the author of evil in the world; yet nevertheless he is executing and achieving all his holy will.

This again is something which is very difficult for our finite minds to comprehend. How can it possibly be that God controls all things and yet our choices are significant? How can it possibly be that God governs all things absolutely, yet is not the author of evil? The theologian Don Carson has put his finger on the reason for our inability to understand. He brings it back to that profound distance between the finite and the infinite, the created and the Creator: 'There is an unbridgeable ontological gap between the personal transcendent God and finite man, and this gap brings about the breakdown of all analogical arguments designed to picture the mode of divine causation.'[2] We understand things by analogy. But there are no complete analogies *within* creation for the way the infinite Creator rules *over* creation.

The Scriptures teach man's responsibility and also God's sovereignty. 'His kingdom is an eternal dominion; his kingdom endures from generation to generation. All the peoples of the earth are regarded as nothing. He does as he pleases with the powers of heaven and the peoples of the earth. No one can hold back his hand or say to him: "What have you done?"' (Daniel 4:34,35). God is God Almighty, the King of kings and Lord of lords.

The Bible, then, paints a picture of God on the most vast canvas. The picture is awe-inspiring, tremendous in the true meaning of that word. He is God, who was and is and is to come, the origin and sustainer of all that exists, the exquisite beautiful fountain of all that is love and that is good, the alpha and omega, the First and Last!

Having sketched out some of the main teachings which Scripture contains concerning God, we must now ask, 'Why believe in God?' and in particular, 'Why believe in the God of the Bible?'

We have to proceed carefully. First of all, as a Christian I have to say that I do not believe in God because I can prove his existence in the way in which we normally think of proof. The Bible nowhere attempts any deductive or philosophical proof for the existence of God, and it does not do so for a very good reason.

When we seek to prove something in logic or mathematics we do so by accepting a certain number of things to be true to begin with. In geometry, for example, these things which we take as certain we call axioms. Then we seek to show that what we are trying to prove follows as a logical necessity from our axioms. But if what the Bible says is true, that God himself is the fountain of everything else in the universe, including us, our minds and even the laws of logic, then there is no foundation more ultimate than him from which we can begin our argument concerning his existence. Thus we cannot go about proving God by the usual route. His unique relationship to the world makes it impossible.

The Christian writer Michael Green sums up the position like this: 'To demonstrate conclusively that God exists, you would have to find something more ultimate than him, from which his existence could be shown to be necessarily derived. And that is, from the very nature of the case, impossible; for God is *the* ultimate.'[3]

So the Bible indicates that it is futile to attempt a formal proof of God's existence in this way. And in fact, if someone could produce such a proof, Christians would have to stop believing in the God of the Bible. If you could prove him, you would have disproved him! The fact is that God as described in Scripture can neither be proved nor disproved in this way, by the very nature of the relationship which he bears to the universe.

But having made this clear does not at all mean that we are unable to get anywhere with our question, nor that God has to be accepted or rejected arbitrarily. The Bible never calls for blind faith.

In fact the apostle Paul states boldly that God's existence is much more obvious than proof. He writes that 'What may be known about God is plain . . . because God has made it plain . . . For since the creation of the world God's invisible qualities – his eternal power and divine nature – have been clearly seen, being understood from what has been made, so that men are without excuse' (Romans 1:19,20). Paul's strident declaration is that unbelief is culpable because when we look at reality, when we contemplate the world in which we live, the fact of God is obvious. He is saying that the basic assumptions of biblical Christianity alone are adequate to describe and understand reality. Reality, the world in which we live, can be thought of as a lock, and there is a bunch of keys, which are all the different ideologies, religions and philosophies of the world, but Christianity is the only key that fits.

Paul explains that men might seek to deny this. He speaks about them 'suppressing the truth' (Romans 1:18) and their reasons for doing that are less than honourable and fall short of integrity. But though they deny it the fact of God is right there in front of them, as plain as the nose on your face. That is Paul's sweeping claim. The fact of God's existence is a lot more obvious and far more certain than perhaps we have ever realized. Christianity makes sense, the God of the Bible makes sense, when nothing else does.

How then do we know that God is there, that Christianity is true? Paul's answer is, because it cannot possibly be otherwise. Let us try to get behind his thinking, by looking at a few different areas of reality.

Knowledge

Suppose, for example, we consider the area of knowledge – how we know things and how we know that we know them. Let us, for the sake of argument, consider some event or object which we will call X.

The Christian is able to be sure of two very important things. First, he has a reason for believing that there is such a thing as *the* truth, in this case the truth about X. The truth exists in the mind of the all-knowing, infinite Creator God who is aware of every detail and every possible aspect of everything, including X. God is the ultimate arbiter therefore of what is true and what is false, and the truth exists.

The second thing is that the Christian has reason to believe that although, because he is a finite human being, he may not know every possible thing that is true about X, nevertheless he can know true things about X because God has made man's mind and perception of things to correspond to reality.* When we see something, we see what is actually there. The image in our mind corresponds with reality, because God has made us that way. Thus the Christian has a basis for knowledge and truth.

But the person who excludes God is in a rather different and difficult situation when he seeks to find a basis for truth and knowledge. Firstly, he is committed to his own independence. He makes himself, not God, the arbiter of truth. But unlike God he is a finite and limited human being. He has to concede therefore that such a thing as *the* truth can never be known to exist. Other people, for example, may perceive X differently from himself. There is then no such thing as the truth. There is only 'This is the way I happen to see it, but you may see it differently.' To exclude God is rather like rubbing out the axes on a graph: you no longer know where you are or even which direction is which. There is no longer absolute truth; there is only relative truth.

However, that leaves the person in an impossible situation because:

1.   If you say that there is no such thing as *the* truth, that

is to make an absolute statement of truth. It is to say, 'It is absolutely true that there is no such thing as absolute truth,' which is self-contradictory. Or,

2. The alternative is to accept that we cannot know anything at all for certain – we can't even know that there isn't absolute truth. This is to be totally uncertain of anything and thus to abandon the possibility of knowing anything at all for certain, and thus of proving anything.

Similarly, the person who rejects God is in great difficulty about knowing whether or not what goes on in his mind corresponds to reality. The person without God is committed to his own independency as the arbiter of truth, but he can never know whether or not he touches the real world unless he accepts that his mind has been designed to correspond to reality. For example, Bertrand Russell said, 'In one sense it must be admitted that we can never prove the existence of things other than ourselves and our experiences. No logical absurdity results from the hypothesis that the world consists of myself and my thoughts and feelings and sensations, and that everything else is mere fancy . . . There is no logical impossibility in the presupposition that the whole of life is a dream in which we ourselves create all the objects that come before us. But although this is not logically impossible there is no reason whatever to suppose it is true; and it is in fact a less simple hypothesis viewed as a means of accounting for the facts of life, than the common-sense hypothesis that the objects are really there.'[4] The only difficulty with Russell's saying that it is a 'less simple' hypothesis is that it does not actually remove the problem, for he has no way of knowing or proving that his idea of 'less simple' corresponds to reality either. The common-sense approach is what we obviously accept. But the person who does not accept a Creator, who has made man's mind and reality to correspond, has no reason with which he can defend the common-sense

position. If he was logically consistent he would have
to admit total uncertainty.

These are fundamental uncertainties which lie at the
bottom of all philosophies which are committed to the
idea that man alone and reason alone are the final arbit-
ers of truth.

Yet, of course, people do not live their lives in total
uncertainty. We live our lives as if the world is real and
not just in our minds (although we cannot prove it). We
live our lives as if knowledge is certain. Thus we feel free
to criticize other people and tell them that they have got
their facts wrong – although all those things can only be
taken as certain in a theistic system, a system of thought
which acknowledges that God is.

This, according to Paul, is part of man's basic sin of
'suppressing the truth' (Romans 1:18). All the time we
live our lives as if God is there, but all the time we deny
it is true. Man is a living self-contradiction.

The great Christian philosopher Cornelius van Til
sums it up like this: 'The proof of the Christian position
is that unless its truth is presupposed, there is no possibility of "proving" anything at all.'[5]

We are driven in a similar direction if we consider the
area of morality.

Morals

How do we know that God is, and thus that Christianity's basic assumptions are true? The answer is
because Christianity is the only way to make sense of
reality in the area of morals, of right and wrong.

Suppose we look at Christianity's two great opponents, Eastern religion and Western humanism. In both
these life-views there is a common assumption which
leads on into other implications for morality. They both
say that reality, pushed back to its foundations, is *imper-*

sonal. They both say that there is no personal God. Let us see where that assumption leads.

Eastern religion

The biblical view of the universe is, as we have seen earlier, that all reality proceeded originally from the personal God. The Bible opens with the words: 'In the beginning God . . .' (Genesis 1:1). Man is made in the image of God. Man is personal, because God is personal. And indeed God is so personal that the infinite God became man in Jesus Christ. So the biblical idea is that the world derives from the personal God who created it.

Eastern religions, however, like Hinduism and Buddhism, deny this. They teach that the ultimate reality is the One. The river of life dissolves into the sea of oblivion, absorbed into the whole, Brahman, the one all-pervading reality. At bottom then, Eastern thought sees everything as one without distinction. Yes, there may be a multiplicity of gods, such as Vishnu and Shiva etc., but these are not ultimate reality; they are simply emanations of the ultimate. At bottom everything is one.

In the Hindu philosophy there is no contradiction between belief in an all-embracing, omnipresent One and the worship of a variety of gods and goddesses in the Hindu pantheon. In religious ceremonies the images of gods may help to focus devotion, but in theory they represent nothing more than imaginative pictures of the infinite aspects of the all-pervading, absolute One.

What flows from this is that ultimately there is no difference between good and evil, between right and wrong, because finally everything is one. It is said that when the soul reaches its true self, morality is transcended. Taken to its logical conclusion this means that the possibility of morality is denied.

Let us consider an example of how this works out.

Not too many years ago in California a horrific and infamous series of murders was carried out by Charles Manson. At the time of his trial, Professor Zhaener, a professor of world religions at Oxford, said some things about the influence of Eastern thought on Manson which caused a stir, but which spell out the implications. A newspaper report of his remarks ran as follows: 'Hindu texts make no bones that the coming to the absolute meant transcending good and evil. Professor Zhaener went on: "Whether Charles Manson had direct access to the original texts I do not know, but that his philosophy was largely based on them, as filtered down to him by the various semi-oriental sects with which he was in contact in the Los Angeles area, seems fairly certain. According to one Hindu text, 'The man who knows me [Brahman] as I am loses nothing that is his whatever he does, even though he should slay his father and mother . . . whatever he does he does not blanch.'" Manson, as Professor Zhaener sharply pointed out, did not blanch. On the absolute plane, killing and being killed were equally unreal. Once you have got rid of all sense of ego you will find that you can murder to your heart's content and feel no remorse.'[6]

The idea of Eastern thought is that man's greatest need is to come to the One and so to transcend time and change and all the opposites which supposedly bedevil human existence and make it so wearisome and complicated. But to come to the One is to transcend good and evil as well. However, to say that is to say that we cannot condemn the murderer like Charles Manson. To say that is to say that right is ultimately the same as wrong, so you cannot have a basis for law and morality in society. Pantheism, which says that everything is God, must ultimately also come to the same conclusions for the same reasons. If all the universe is God, then evil is as much part of God as good.

Now, obviously, society could not live like that for a

moment. It would be terrifying chaos. The whole of experience testifies against such an outlook on life. Eastern religion gives no basis for the morality which is so obviously essential to human life. A universe without morality is a universe divorced from reality.

Western humanism

Similarly Western humanism is unable to provide a proper basis for morality. The Western outlook is governed by a materialistic scientific approach to the universe. Everything ultimately is impersonal. The universe consists of simply matter and energy and time and chance. Human personality can be reduced to biology, physics and chemistry.

Highly complex chemical processes are all that we are. Love is one such process in our brains. Hate is another. But how can we say that a chemical reaction is a responsible moral entity? How can a chemical reaction, be it in a test-tube or in a human brain, be right or wrong? It cannot. You cannot derive morality from a fundamentally impersonal universe. The possibility of morality is once again denied.

Indeed in the context of a merely evolutionary outlook to life, morality is a positive disadvantage. In his book *The Selfish Gene,* Richard Dawkins puts the logic of a godless world very clearly: 'The world of the gene machine is one of savage competition, ruthless exploitation and deceit . . . I shall argue that a predominant quality to be expected in a successful gene is selfishness in individual behaviour. However, as we shall see there are special circumstances in which a gene can achieve its own ends best by fostering a limited form of altruism, at the level of individual animals. "Special" and "limited" are important words in the last sentence. Much as we may wish to believe otherwise, universal love and the welfare of the species as a whole are concepts which simply do not make evolutionary sense.'[7] Without God we are left with the logic of the survival of the fittest and with the rightness of all the rivalry, violence and misery that implies.

Here we have come face to face with man's fundamental perversity. All through our lives we invoke a moral code for others. When a thief assaults us and steals our belongings we do not sit down and say, as we should if we believed the survival of the fittest was right, 'Well he was stronger than I am, so that makes his action acceptable.' That kind of thinking does not enter our heads.

All the time we live as if there is a real morality. We are indignant and outraged by the thief, the rapist and the murderer. We condemn other people who have been selfish or dishonest. We declare some people right in what they have done and others wrong, and by that we mean more than that their actions were more or less expedient.

We do these things, but all the time we insist on a world-view without God, which denies the possibility of morality, of 'right' and 'wrong' having any meaning. Only if reality is the creation of the personal holy God whose righteous character is the definition of what is right, does morality make sense.

We are back again to Paul's claim in Romans 1 that man assumes a framework to life which only makes sense if God is there, yet all the time he ignores God and seeks to deny his existence.

The best that Western humanism can do to construct a morality is to set up law by consensus. But that is inherently unjust, since 'right' and 'wrong' can simply change with a majority vote. What is wrong one day can be 'right' the next, according to variations in public opinion.

An impersonal universe cannot hold any ultimate morality. As my wife's philosophy tutor at university used to say, 'You cannot get an "ought" from an "is".' In this matter of morality only the personal God makes sense of life.

Let me put it all another way. If there is not a loving person behind the universe, then as we have seen from Richard Dawkins's logic, love does not make sense, especially self-sacrificial love. But we all know that without love we paint a totally inadequate picture of reality. Love is one of the most powerful forces in the world. There is a film entitled *The Elephant Man,* made in 1980, starring the actor John Hurt. It illustrates the power of love and kindness. The film tells the true story of a man called John Merrick who lived in England in the last century. Due to some illness of his mother in pregnancy, John Merrick was born unspeakably deformed. He became known as the Elephant Man. Poor John Merrick was an outcast in society; rejected and mistreated, he retreated into himself as a personality. He never spoke and it was imagined that he was senseless and dumb. He was eventually 'owned' by a man who ran a grotesque side-show in a fair-ground. People would come and pay for the cheap thrill of seeing the horrific sight of the Elephant Man. There Merrick lived, often starved and beaten.

At last, initially out of medical fascination, a doctor began to show an interest in the Elephant Man. The film shows, very movingly, that as the doctor began to extend to Merrick a little kindness and respect, this man, whom many had looked upon as an animal, began to respond. He began to learn to read and to speak. In an atmosphere of compassion and love it was not long before it became obvious that beneath that monstrous exterior lived a most lovely and intelligent human being in whom other people could take delight. A complete transformation in John Merrick took place as he blossomed as a personality and began to take delight in other people and the arts. It was a transformation which occurred simply due to the power of love.

But John Merrick's case is only a very striking example of a common phenomenon in our world. Love causes people to flourish. Love changes people and situations for good. Love is a very potent part of reality, and to deny that is to deny what is obvious.

However, without God, there is no rationale for love. The God of love being there at the back of reality alone makes sense of love. To love makes sense because it is to follow the Maker's pattern, it is to be in tune with the ultimate reality.

If, at bottom, the universe is only the impersonal One of Eastern thought, or the matter-energy-time-chance interplay of the Western world-view, then there can be no basis for love. In an impersonal universe there can be no morality, for good and evil are the same, love is the same as hate.

But by our own experience we know that is not the case. Love is not the same as hate. These other world-views are perpetrating a lie. Christianity alone can make sense of our experience of the world. Once again we see Paul's basic contention that the fact of God is plain. Though people may choose to deny it, God is a lot more obvious than 'proof'. He alone explains the world we know; he alone is the key which fits the lock of reality.

To summarize then, so far, I do not claim to have 'proved' the existence of God in the classic sense, because unless some assumptions, some axioms, are accepted by faith at the start of any reasoning process, reason cannot begin. I have argued that only the assumption of the God of Scripture is big enough to make sense of the world we know.

We are not to be rude, but there is no need for the Christian to be over-apologetic or hesitant about his or her faith. Christianity is not asking anyone to throw away their minds or bury their brains in becoming a Christian. Christianity provides a robust and perfectly defensible view of the world. The Christian affirmation

'I believe in God the Father Almighty . . .' seems to be an eminently sensible creed.

But before we leave this subject two other considerations are worth reflecting on.

Prophecy

Although the Bible never constructs a purely logical argument for God, it does argue for God very powerfully by another route. The Bible contains sixty-six books, which were written over a period of some 1600 years, and is the work, humanly speaking, of some forty different authors. It records God's dealings with people over a vast period of time, from the origin of man, through his espousing of the nation of Israel as his people in the Old Testament, right through to the coming of Christ and the inception of the world-wide church blossoming throughout the first-century Roman empire. As it progresses, recounting and commenting upon the history of God's people, we find a great deal of prediction about the future. Prophecy, foretelling coming events, is a thread which runs throughout the story, and all the time encourages the reader of the Bible to recognize the hand of God guiding and shaping the contours of history. Some of this prediction is fairly obscure and hard to understand, but much of it is very straightforward. Indeed, looking at the Bible story as a whole, it seems that the next stage in the development of major events is usually foretold. More often than not, there is a bridge of prophecy which reaches forward into the future. The Scriptures claim that God is the Lord of history, and that he shows himself to be just that through his revealing of the future to his prophets.

Here are some examples of this from the Old Testament: Abraham was chosen by God, when he and his wife Sarah were without children, and were infertile; yet

God promised to make him the father of a great nation, the Jews. God also promised Abraham that his descendants would possess the land of Palestine, but made plain that before that happened they would be slaves in a foreign land (Genesis 12:2,3; 15:13-18). These things came about as the family of Abraham's grandson, Jacob, moved to Egypt in time of famine, there increased greatly in numbers, but over the years fell into slavery. The events of Israel's escape from Egypt and move to the promised land under the leadership of Moses, beginning at the Exodus, are well known.

Just before entering the promised land Moses reiterated God's laws, and warned Israel of the consequences of disobeying God. He predicted that disobedience would issue in the nation losing the promised land and being taken away into captivity again (Deuteronomy 28:36,64). After many hundreds of years, as the nation of Israel strayed further and further from God, this is precisely what happened, as the Jews went into captivity in Babylon during the sixth century B.C.

But again, through such prophets as Isaiah and Jeremiah, who lived during the eighth and seventh centuries B.C. respectively, God revealed that not only would the Jews go into exile, but that Babylon would be destroyed and they would return from exile, Jeremiah specifying a period of seventy years for the captivity (e.g. Isaiah 48:12-22; Jeremiah 25:11-12). All this happened when Cyrus, King of Persia, overcame Babylon and sent home its captive peoples (2 Chronicles 36:20-23).

Of course, many people, including modern critics, having rejected God and the supernatural, do not accept the possibility of such predictions and therefore seek to explain away such prophecies by claiming that in fact they were written *after* the events.† However, three things need to be realized.

1.   Very often little or no evidence can be produced to

support the supposed later dates of authorship of such
prophecies, apart from the tacit assumption that the
later date must be true because such prediction is impossible *a priori*. This reflects the critic's personal
world-view, or 'faith' commitment, rather than the
actual evidence.

2.   This approach assumes that the majority of the biblical writers were either complete idiots or the most dishonest charlatans, frequently condemning lying as a sin,
yet quite happy to perpetrate lies in their writings, claiming them to be written many years previously and by
other people.

3.   But, be these things as they may, there remains a
large collection of biblical prophecy which simply cannot
be dismissed so readily. For example, the Old Testament prophets and the psalms do seem to speak plainly
of the birth and sufferings of the Messiah in quite
remarkable detail, and were fulfilled in the life of Jesus
in a way which could not have been contrived (e.g.
Psalm 22:16; Micah 5:2; Isaiah 7:14; 53: 3-12). All the
Old Testament was certainly written 300 years before
Christ. A copy of the book of Isaiah was found among
the Dead Sea scrolls and is dated by scholars as being
from the second century B.C.

Again the Old Testament prophets often predict the
spread of the worship of the God of Israel into all the
world following the coming of the Messiah. The Gospels
and other New Testament writings confidently predict
the same thing. And with the spread of the Christian
faith throughout the world, who is to say that they were
wrong? (Revelation 7:9).

Although it carries a message of forgiveness and love
to the world, throughout its long history the church, as it
has remained faithful to the New Testament teachings,
has always been, in one form or another, a suffering,
persecuted church. Recently, Michael Bordeaux has
written, 'Bold would be the man who claimed that fewer

than two million Christians have given up their life for the faith in this century.'[8] Countless others are imprisoned or socially and educationally penalized for their faith. This again is all spelt out in advance by the New Testament. Jesus said to his followers, 'Remember the words I spoke to you: "No servant is greater than his master." If they persecuted me, they will persecute you also. If they obeyed my teaching, they will obey yours also' (John 15:20). Paul, the apostle to the Gentiles, writes, 'In fact, everyone who wants to live a godly life in Christ Jesus will be persecuted' (2 Timothy 3:12). Christians know what that is about, from the cold shoulder and derogatory remarks among family and workmates, right down to the labour camps of totalitarian regimes.

Much more could be said on this topic, but this prophetic witness does seem to point to the reality of God, and to the fact that the God who exists is the God of the Bible.

Science

Another area in which it is hard not to see the hand of God is that of the creation itself. Referring once again to Romans 1, the apostle Paul writes that 'Since the creation of the world God's invisible qualities – his eternal power and divine nature – have been clearly seen, being understood from what has been made, so that men are without excuse' (Romans 1:20).

When considering the origins of the universe, of our world, of life etc., it has been fashionable among scientists for nearly a couple of centuries to rest their case on the operations of chance events, in order to try to explain the present arrangement of things. Starting, as reductionist science has to, with the most elementary building blocks, chance is the only available tool of explanation in the supposedly closed universe. However, there are two considerations which ought to be weighed, without going into great scientific technicalities.

1. It is surely true that anything which is supposedly explained by a chance event can equally well be explained by design. The fact that when we spin a penny in the air, it can land either heads or tails, by chance, does not mean that every penny we come across *must* have landed the way up it has, by chance. It could just as easily have been placed where it is, and the way it is, by design. Similarly, all the configurations of the basic constituents of the universe can equally well be explained by design as well as by chance. In this sense science can never 'disprove' God.

Now, at that point, the outlook of scientific materialism would perhaps agree, but would say that the chance explanation is a more simple explanation, bringing God into things is an unnecessary complication, and we should always opt for the most simple explanations.

However, this brings us to our second consideration. Can it really be defended that the constant invocation of chance provides the simplest explanation?

2. Someone has put it like this. Have you ever played cards against someone who cheats? After they have dealt themselves an unbeatable hand for the fifth time running, you probably said something like, 'I can believe in flukes, so long as they don't happen too often!' Godless science wants to explain everything by chance, by flukes. That is fine, but I feel I have to say that I can believe in flukes so long as they do not happen too often.

Suppose for the sake of argument that we divide up the material world into five sections or strata, as follows:

Fundamental universal laws - F
Inorganic matter   - F + w
Plant life   - F + w + x
Animal life   - F + w + x + y
Human life   - F + w + x + y + z

Each one of these levels can be seen to include something qualitatively different from the level preceding it. Inorganic matter is more than a law or principle. Plant life is more than inorganic rock and dust etc. The extra ingredients we have labelled w,x,y,z.

Now, for the Christian who believes in the Creator, there is no problem with this. But for the atheist, each one of the jumps w,x,y,z to the next level must be explained as a chance event, often against the most literally incredible odds. Furthermore, within each level of existence chance has to be relied upon again and again. If, for example, we look at our own planet, even at the inorganic level, the fact that although there are many stars in the universe of greatly varying sizes, ages and states of stability, yet we just happen to have a nice, middle-aged, friendly one at the centre of our solar system is by chance. The fact that our planet is at just the right distance from the sun, so as to make it neither too hot nor too cold, is by chance. The fact that our planet's size is such that gravity is neither so great as to crush, nor too little so as not to be able to retain atmosphere, is by chance. Again, the helpful rotational period of the planet is neither too slow, so as to cause impossible temperature variations, nor too fast so as to cause impossible cyclonic conditions; that also is a chance situation.[9] This continual turning to chance just goes on and on and as yet we have not even begun to talk about the chances surrounding the actual origin of life, the so-called 'primeval soup', nor the chances involved in the theories of the evolution of all the species by possible mutations in genetic material.

No, many people feel that although they can believe in flukes, they have to happen far too often, and against far too great odds, for the chance explanation of the universe to be true. The account of chance is overdrawn at the bank of credibility. In many ways the French eighteenth-century philosopher Montesquieu voiced in its most pointed form this doubt in the chance explanation, even before the debate really got going in later years. He wrote, 'Those who have said that blind fatality has produced all the effects that we see in the world have uttered a great absurdity; for what greater absurdity than a blind fatality which has produced intelligent beings?'[10]

The idea that the chance explanation of reality is a more simple theory and therefore a more credible theory is open to grave doubt.

Many would say that, looking at the universe, they see the hand of design, not the blind stumblings of chance.‡

We have looked briefly at the central feature of Christian faith, the fact of God, and much more could be said. To summarize this chapter then, we have seen that, perhaps contrary to popular opinion, there is much to commend the Christian view of the world as God's creation. Faith in God does not rest on the conclusion of a long chain of tentative argument. The case for God is very plain. Unless God is presupposed, we are unable to understand reality, we have no key to the world. That the universe has a personal rather than an impersonal origin alone makes sense of our everyday experience of life.

It is therefore worth reminding ourselves again that the New Testament's first answer as to why we should believe is simply because Christianity is true, and to reject it is to 'suppress the truth'.

*The reality which we perceive is a subset of total reality and total reality may be equated with God's knowledge.

†It is true that some prophecies were actually committed to writing after the events themselves. In particular, if Moses wrote the book of Genesis this is the case with the references to Abraham. But this does not mean that Abraham was not given them in advance.

‡For example, Paul Davies, a leading professor of theoretical physics in Britain, has said, in *New Scientist* magazine, 'Modern physics has shown that there is something truly extraordinary about the way the laws of physics fit together, the way the universe has been put together. It is not just any old universe; it is a very special, fine-tuned arrangement of things.' Elsewhere he has written, 'The laws of physics dovetail together with such exquisite consistency and coherence that the impression of design is overwhelming.' Professor Davies is not a Christian, but just looking at the evidence he is saying that the universe shows obvious signs of having been planned, and plan or design must speak of a designer, God.

References

1. Bertrand Russell, *Autobiography*, Unwin, 1975.
2. Don Carson, *Divine Sovereignty and Human Responsibility*, Marshalls, 1981.
3. Michael Green, *Choose Freedom*, IVP, p.14.
4. Bertrand Russell, *Problems of Philosophy*, Oxford University Press, p.10.
5. Cornelius van Til quoted from interview in *Christianity Today*.
6. Quoted by Ranald MacAuley in lecture 'How de we know that Christianity is true?' given at the Millmead Centre, Guildford, 1984.
7. Richard Dawkins, *The Selfish Gene*, Paladin, 1976.
8. Michael Bordeaux in preface to H. B. Workman's *Persecution in the Early Church*, Oxford University Press, 1980.
9. Alan Hayward, *Does God Exist?* Lakeland, 1983.
10. Quoted by J. Bronowski and B. Mazlish, *The Western Intellectual Tradition*, Penguin Books, 1963, p.311.

3.
But Jesus lived so long ago

One of the most exciting stories that I can remember reading in my younger days was H. G. Wells's classic novel *The Time Machine*. What a wonderfully adventurous and romantic idea, to be able to travel in time; to be projected into the future to see what will happen; to go back into the past and view at first hand the epic events and the great men and women who have shaped the course of history!

But, of course, this is all science *fiction*. Time travel is not possible. For us history remains the great irretrievable, the great inaccessible. The simple wish to 'have our time over again' is an impossible dream. Man, with his wisdom and skill, has opened up access to nearly every single part of the world. Even outer space is becoming accessible to us. But the one immense doorway which is for ever shut to our direct experience is in the dimension of time. We have no direct access to either the future or the past.

Christianity has to do with history. We have already considered something of the reasoning for belief in God. But Christianity is not just about God. It is about Jesus Christ. It is *Christ*ianity. It is claiming that the God who exists has made himself known in Christ.

Thus we need to ask about Jesus Christ and when we do that we must ask about history. Jesus it is claimed, is a figure of history. How can we be sure that we have the facts about Jesus Christ? What is the historical evidence concerning him? We now come to look at such questions.

In the last chapter I argued that in fact the Christian is the only person who has a proper basis for knowledge. It is only the Christian who can be sure that reality exists and that people are capable of perceiving true things about reality. To be consistent therefore, I should really now argue that unless we accept the Christian explanation of the world to begin with, we have no foundation for the study of history.

However, I realize that that is not where most people reading this book will be in their thinking and therefore in this chapter I try to argue that even if we approach history with a non-Christian outlook, nevertheless Christian faith makes historical sense.

As we have said, we have no direct access to the past. That being the case, trying to start our thinking where most folk would start, we have to realize that matters of history can never be examined or proved in the same way as matters of science or mathematics. The very foundations of scientific method and investigation are the ideas of direct observation and repeatable experiment. A scientific law is established as experiments to verify that law can be set up by any investigator and observed as many times as we like and the same results reproduced. By very definition such a method is impossible with matters of history. We cannot fling ourselves back into history and directly observe events. Science is directly observable and repeatable. History is neither of those things. Even when we talk of 'history repeating itself', we do not mean that precisely the same event has occurred twice (what would 'twice' mean in this context?) – we are speaking figuratively. We cannot travel back in time. A historian is someone who finds out today what happened yesterday! We can only investigate history in a second-hand way by evidence which may have come down to us.

Because of this, we have to say that, taking the common view of knowledge, matters of history can never be established with the same degree of certainty as matters of science. Even a film of an event in the past cannot do that. How do we know that this film is a film of the event it purports to be? How do we know whether or not the film has been edited or shot from a particular perspective in order to convey the truth about the event in an unbiased fashion? We can never be absolutely sure. History, as it is popularly conceived, by its very nature can never deal in complete certainty, only in high probabilities.

Starting where most people start their thinking, then, we must not ask for the historicity of Jesus to be proved with the certainty of a mathematical equation. This cannot be done for any event in the distant past. Rather, within the terms of the certainty within which the popular way of thinking can be sure about anything in distant history, we will ask, 'Does faith in Christ have a reasonable basis in history?'

An open mind

As we approach looking at the historical evidence concerning Jesus from the popular point of view, one thing has to be faced head on. In the life of Christ we are looking at something which claims to be absolutely unique, totally without parallel. This inevitably presents a problem to some historians. It does so because of a fundamental assumption which underlies some modern approaches to history. This assumption we call the principle of analogy or precedent. History is assumed to be a closed continuum of material cause and effect in which nothing truly exceptional ever happens. With this assumption in mind, a man called Lee Simpson has said with tongue in cheek, 'Any event, once it has occurred, can be made to seem inevitable by a competent historian!'

But making this assumption that history is a closed continuum, the conclusion is then drawn that since this is the case, the type of events witnessed or experienced in past ages must be of the same type that we witness now, perhaps described in more primitive language, but qualitatively exactly the same. (The ancients might describe a particular cataclysm as a judgement from heaven; we would describe it as a volcano erupting, etc.) When this conclusion has been reached a decision is then taken about what kinds of things are accepted as historical evidence. The principle of analogy says that only if we have knowledge of something similar before, or of something parallel happening in our own experience, can an event be believed to have occurred. The event must be analogous to other well-known events, or have a precedent in another well-attested event, before we can look upon the report of it as admissible evidence.

The problem with this approach to history is that it can never cope with any unique event, and when we come to consider Christ we are inevitably considering something which claims to be unique. The principle of analogy can never cope with anything which has only happened once and of which the historian has no experience.

But if what is claimed for Christ is true, there never has been, and never could be, a life like his anywhere else in history. He is the Son of God, without precedent. The last three years of his life on earth, it is claimed, are surrounded on every side by miracles and culminate in the ultimate miracle of resurrection from the dead. The principle of analogy must reject this out of hand. Modern historians have never come across anything parallel to this. To adopt the principle of analogy would therefore be to reject Christianity before we even begin to consider it.

But there are three things which need to be said about the principle of analogy. The *first* is that its primary concern is that it is seeking to guard against falsehood being perpetrated as fact, and that concern is obviously immensely important. Made-up stories must not be allowed to pass as historical fact. However, there are better ways of safeguarding the truth than by making a blanket supposition of what will and what will not be accepted as evidence, which is what the principle of analogy amounts to.

The *second* is that to assume history to be a closed continuum of cause and effect, and that therefore such things as miracles and the incarnation of the Son of God are not possible, is actually an atheistic presupposition. It therefore cooks the books before investigation begins. As we have seen from chapter 2, atheism is hardly a certain assumption. Surely, no one has the right to impose what amounts to an unquestionable presupposition which will govern the selection of which evidence will be admissible. It is to come to the court and say, 'We will recognize as evidence only those things that support our position.' Hardly fair!

The *third* thing which needs to be seen is that the principle of analogy is parallel to making the limits of one's own experience the limits of what is possible. It is the attitude which says, 'I have never seen a miracle, so therefore miracles do not happen.' But that is to have a closed mind. Because you have never seen a miracle, it doesn't mean that other people haven't. Remember the story of the old missionary in the nineteenth century telling South Sea Islanders of the sea being turned to ice and people being able to walk over it. They laughed him to scorn, simply because it was something beyond their experience. Point taken?

As we approach the evidence concerning Christ, then, we must realize that we are looking at something which is totally without parallel and the only thing that is asked is that it is approached without disposing of it as impossible before we start. If God exists, it is not surprising that remarkable things can happen, especially as he unfolds his plan of salvation. Do not prejudge the issue. All that is asked is an open mind. The great claim of Christianity is that, approaching the evidence with an open mind, Christianity is seen to be historically true. It is asserted that there is as much, if not more, evidence for Christ and for Christian faith, as for any other fact of history which we would accept without question.

Here are four considerations which point to the historical truth of Christ.

1. The quality of the story

The first point which is worth bearing in mind is the quality of the story of Jesus. If it is not true, then somehow and for some purpose it must have been invented by people who wanted it to be believed. But this story just does not bear the marks of a tale that has been invented in order to gather a following among people.

David Kingdon has put this very well. Remarking on the virgin birth he writes, 'You do not invent a story about an engaged woman conceiving a child and claiming that no man was involved. Scripture assures us that Mary was a virgin before the conception of Jesus and a virgin until after he was born. You do not invent such a story if you want the Gospel to gain easy acceptance among Jews, for they held pre-marital chastity in such high regard that a woman could be stoned to death if proved to have been unchaste before marriage. The virgin birth is so clearly a black mark against Mary and Joseph – and our Lord himself – that the really incredible thing is to believe that the early church invented the idea! Nor do you invent such a story if you want the Gospel message to carry conviction in the Gentile world among non-Jews. To speak generally, the Gentiles were at the opposite end of the spectrum to the Jews. Among them chastity was held in little regard. So a story of a virgin who conceived without sexual relations would simply invite ribald jokes! Such a story has got to be true or there is no point in it whatsoever.'[1]

A similar line of argument could equally be used concerning the death of Christ on the cross. To invent a story that they had rejected and crucified their Messiah was hardly the way to curry favour with the Jewish nation, and to speak of a Saviour who was led as a beaten captive to the cross and done to death was surely not the currency with which to win a popular following in the raw, hard-bitten atmosphere of the first-century Roman Gentile world. It was just as the apostle Paul declared: 'We preach Christ crucified: a stumbling-block to Jews and foolishness to Gentiles' (1 Corinthians 1:23). Paul realized that what he preached had no natural appeal. It was not 'invented' with that purpose. If it had been, the inventor had obviously done a very bad job.

Again, the miracles and the story of the resurrection of Christ are not, and never have been, things which are easily believable. When Paul was at Athens and preached the good news of Christianity, the book of Acts records, 'When they heard about the resurrection of the dead, some of them sneered . . .' (Acts 17:32), and many have sneered ever since.

So we can see that there is a good case for saying that, whatever it is, the story of Christ hardly bears the marks of something which was invented in order to get a following among people. It is too 'incredible' to have been invented. In this way there is an element of self-authentification in the story of Jesus. Here, immediately, is a *prima facie* case for the truth of it.

2. The quality of the opposition

To really establish the truth of something we need to be
critical. We must not just accept everything we hear, but
we must test it, try it. Therefore, secondly, it is particularly worth looking at Jesus by considering what people
who were not Christians, but who were around at the
time that Christianity was getting off the ground, said
about Christ and Christian faith. What did the enemies
of Christianity say about it?

There are a number of references to Christianity in
the works of ancient authors. Mention is made of it in the
works of some of the Roman writers. For example,
Pliny, a Roman proconsul in what is modern-day
Turkey, wrote to his emperor Trajan in about A.D. 110,
asking for advice about how to deal with Christians and
his letter has come down to us.

The Jewish historian Josephus, writing about A.D.
94, just sixty years after Christ's crucifixion, refers to
Jesus. He says this: 'At this time there was a wise man
called Jesus. And his conduct was good and known to be
virtuous. And many people from among the Jews
became his disciples. Pilate condemned him to be
crucified and to die. And those who became his disciples
did not abandon his discipleship. They reported that he
had appeared to them three days after his crucifixion and
that he was alive. Accordingly he was perhaps the
Messiah of whom the prophets have recounted
wonders.'[2]

But two sources of information about Christ from the
ancient world are of particular interest. First, the
Roman historian Tacitus was no lover of Christianity.
He calls it a 'mischievous superstition'. He was also a
man seemingly with access to all the official Roman
archives. Writing in about A.D. 115 concerning Nero's
persecution of Christians in A.D. 64 he speaks of

'Christ, who was executed in the reign of Tiberius, by the procurator Pontius Pilate'.

Secondly, the Jewish traditions called the Mishna and the Gemara, basically minutes of rabbinical meetings from the early centuries A.D., have some very unpleasant things to say about Christ. One of these begins: 'On the eve of the Passover they hanged Yeshu of Nazareth.' But another reads: 'Rabbi Shimeon ben Azzai said . . . "Such an one is a bastard of an adulteress."' And a third records, 'Rabbi Eliezer said, "Balaam looked forth and saw that there was a man, born of woman, who should rise up and seek to make himself God, and to cause the whole world to go astray . . . and he will deceive and say that he departs and comes again at the end."'[3] These and other passages seem to be references to Jesus.

What are we to make of these words of the enemies of Christianity? Well, surely we must say that at the very minimum they form a very solid ground for accepting the fact of Jesus as a figure of history. Tacitus might call Christianity a superstition, but he firmly accepts that Jesus himself lived. From the Jewish references, surely we must conclude that there is no reason at all to doubt the existence of Jesus, for people do not get so worked up and vehemently slander someone who never existed!

Actually these references go a lot further than attesting the mere fact that Jesus lived. They go a long way, once again, to confirming many of the central features of the New Testament accounts of Jesus' life, out of the mouths of those who were Christianity's enemies. He lived, and died under Pontius Pilate. It was claimed that he was alive again and would return.

3. The quality of the documents

We have seen something of what non-Christians of the

time have to say of Christ. But the main sources of information about Jesus are the four Gospels. How reliable are they?

There are three questions to be asked here; *the first* is about how near in time to Jesus the Gospels were written, *the second* is about how purely the original New Testament text has been transmitted down to us today, and *the third* is about how objective the original writers of the New Testament were in recording the facts. Let us comment on each in turn.

1. Sometimes people moot the idea that the Gospels have very little to do with Jesus and were probably written long after the events, perhaps even centuries afterwards.

In considering that idea it is worth quoting from the autobiography of Lord Hailsham, until recently the Lord Chancellor of Great Britain. After a long life in the legal profession he comments on the idea that the Gospels are well removed in time from the events they purport to report, as follows: 'The second reason which renders the argument invalid is a fact which I learned myself in the course of a case I did in which there was in question the authenticity of a painting purporting to be by, and to be signed by, Modigliani. This painting, as the result of my Advice on Evidence, was shown to be a fake by X-ray evidence. But in the course of my researches I was supplied by my instructing solicitor with a considerable bibliography concerning the nature of fakes of all kinds and how to detect them. There was one point made by the author of one of these books which is of direct relevance to the point I am discussing. Although fakes can often be made which confuse or actually deceive contemporaries of the faker, the experts, or even the not so expert, of a later age can invariably detect them, whether fraudulent or not, because the faker cannot fail to include stylistic or even other material not obvious to contemporaries because they are contemporaries, but which stand out a mile to later observers because they reflect the standards, or materials, or the styles of a succeeding age to that of the author whose work is being faked. This is true of pictures and statues and, though less obviously, of written works.

'Now within a very few years of the writing of the Gospels, an immense Christian literature grew up about the life, the manners, the family, the childhood, the nature and alleged miracles of Jesus of Nazareth, some orthodox, some manifestly heretical, some even conceivably containing elements of authenticity. Some of these have been known for a long time. Some have been disinterred during my lifetime. Some go back to the 2nd and 3rd centuries A. D. Some, no doubt, are still waiting in the sands of Egypt for some future scholar to discover, and some may even now be awaiting transcription and translation. They are as different from the authentic tradition as chalk is from cheese. The authentic books fit into a particular time slot (say from 50 to 100 A.D.) and into no other.'[4]

The crucifixion of Jesus took place around the year A.D. 30 and thus there is every reason to believe that the Gospels were written very close to the events which they record.

2. How purely has the original New Testament text been transmitted down to us? Beyond all question the New Testament is the best attested book of ancient times. The number of early manuscripts of the New Testament far exceeds that of any other ancient book and the period between the date of writing and the date of first copies which have survived is far smaller than for any other book.

For example, for Caesar's *Gallic Wars*, written around 60 B.C., there are only some nine or ten good copies, the oldest of which comes from a time some 900

years after Caesar. The writings of Tacitus, whom we
have already had occasion to mention, are known to us
through only two manuscripts, one from the ninth and
the other from the eleventh century A.D.

By gigantic contrast we have some 13,000 copies of
ancient New Testament manuscripts or parts of manuscripts. The earliest portion, the John Rylands manuscript, is part of John's Gospel and is dated around A.D.
130. Other manuscripts range in age from between A.D.
200 and A.D. 500, all of which are comparatively far
earlier than from any other ancient book. There are very
slight variations of wording between some manuscripts.
But there is no major difference and it amounts to 99%
agreement among themselves as to the original text of
the New Testament.

This reliability of the New Testament text should not
at all surprise us. After all, the words of Jesus and of the
apostles were looked upon as the most precious earthly
possession of the early church and obviously great care
was taken to copy and preserve them in all their purity.

Compared with all other ancient literature, we have
every reason to be confident that in the New Testament,
what we have got today is what was originally written.

3. 'But', say some people, 'although the manuscripts
may be well attested, the point at issue is how far their
contents can be explained in terms of the subjective
belief of the early Christians about Jesus, rather than the
objective facts of what he actually did and was like. The
church wrote the New Testament', they say, 'no doubt
based on the man Jesus, but they wrote all kinds of
things about him which they would have liked to believe
about him, rather than what was actually true. They
shaped and embellished the story in order to present it in
the best light, and to relate it to their own situation, and
thereby added things which had no basis in reality. The
Jesus presented in the New Testament is a Jesus

manufactured by a biased church, and has little if anything to do with the truth about Jesus of Nazareth.'

This charge appears very plausible and forces us to consider whether there is a difference between the 'Lord of faith' presented by the New Testament, and the real 'Jesus of history'.

In response, it must first be accepted that the Gospels were indeed written by Christians, partly with an evangelistic intent. But the nub of the accusation against the reliability of the Gospels rests on the tacit assumption that it is not possible for a writer to be enthusiastically in favour of something and yet refrain from exaggeration and untruth. This quite clearly is not a very sound assumption, not least because any sensible person must realize that to be swept into untruth in your enthusiasm for a cause will only have the sure effect of undermining that cause in the long run, once the lie has been exposed. Anyone truly convinced of his cause and who truly wants to promote that cause has a very weighty reason for sticking to nothing but the truth as he knows it.

There is a lot of evidence to suggest that the New Testament writers were wedded to the truth, governed by such considerations as these. Although foolish and devious people may enlist untruth in support of a cause, there are many indications that the New Testament writers, while having a message to promote, took seriously the fact that their message included at its very core the highest possible regard for the sanctity of truth. Jesus had said, 'You will know the truth, and the truth will set you free' (John 8:32).

Here are some of the reasons for thinking that the New Testament writers took seriously the need for truth and objective reporting.

a. The Gospel writers openly record all the failings of the apostles. For example, just taking Mark's Gospel, on

numerous occasions we find Mark recording Jesus
having to rebuke the apostles for their slowness of
understanding and unbelief (Mark 4:40; 8:21; 9:17-19).
Again, Mark records a time when Jesus felt it necessary
to confront Peter with the sharp words: 'Get behind me,
Satan!' (Mark 8:33). Peter's cowardice and denial of
Christ at the time of Jesus' trial are included in the
Gospel for all to see (Mark 14:66-72). Indeed the fact
that all the disciples deserted Jesus when he was arrested
is recorded too (Mark 14:50). The inclusion of such
information is hardly flattering to the initiators of Christianity. Surely, if a writer was seeking to colour up the
story in a way which presented the apostles and the
church in the best light, these are the kind of things he
would have left out.

Similarly, the Gospels also record many of the
nastiest taunts and accusations which were made against
Christ by his enemies. They called him demon-possessed
(Mark 3:22; John 8:52). They called him mentally
deranged (John 10:20). Jesus was called a Samaritan, a
term of racial abuse (John 8:48). To be called 'the son of
Mary' (with no mention of a father) was a way of calling
into question the legitimacy of Christ's birth (Mark 6:3).
Again, surely such things would have qualified for
removal by the editor's pen if the Gospel writers were
more concerned with making Jesus look good, than with
the truth.

b. Scrutiny of the linguistic and grammatical make-up
of the Gospels also seems to indicate that through them
we are brought into direct contact with Jesus as he was.
Consider this. The New Testament was written in the
lingua franca Greek language of the first century. But, of
course, Jesus, being a Jew, spoke in Aramaic, the
common language of the Jews. Different languages have
different rhythms and constructions, different idioms
and different ways of saying things. For example, the

English use of the verbs 'to be' or 'to have', in order to form past and future tenses of other verbs, is not necessary in many other languages. Or again, I do not suppose that 'gone for a Burton' would mean much to an Eskimo, but most English people would understand! Different languages have their own fingerprints.

Occasionally in the Gospels we come across actual Aramaic words left untranslated: words like 'Abba' or 'Golgotha' (Matthew 27:46; Mark 5:41; John 19:13). But, more important still, close study of the Gospels reveals that often Aramaic expressions underlie the Greek construction. Aramaic fingerprints are on the Gospels. In fact it has been shown that if some parts of Jesus' words in the Gospels are translated back into Aramaic you find alliteration and poetry. These things are not present in the Greek, but they are in the Aramaic. This would seem to suggest strongly that the Gospel writers have been very careful to preserve the original teaching of Jesus.

Professor Joachim Jeremias, a pioneer in this kind of study of the Gospel text, has said. 'The linguistic and stylistic evidence shows so much faithfulness and such respect for the sayings of Jesus that we are justified in drawing up the following principle of method: in the synoptic tradition it is the inauthenticity and not the authenticity of the sayings of Jesus that must be demonstrated.'[5] In other words, it seems the burden of proof lies with those who would seek to deny that the Gospels record the authentic teaching of Jesus, not with those who believe the Gospels to be reliable. The assumption that the Gospels are trustworthy is the more natural assumption.

c.   Since the eighteenth century it is surely true to say that no book has ever been subjected to such searching investigation and critical scrutiny as the Bible. But its durability in the face of such often openly hostile attacks

is quite remarkable. One of the most biased and stiffest
of tests applied by critics to the Gospels is known as the
principle of dissimilarity.

This principle assumes that nothing should be considered as authentically from Jesus if it is paralleled either
in Jewish rabbinic sources or in the thought and teaching
of the early church. In practice that would mean that we
should only accept that the real Jesus is seen when what
is recorded goes against Jewish tradition and also
concerns of the early Christians. Now that is plainly
ridiculous because it would mean, first, that Jesus knew
nothing and never quoted anything found in the traditions of his own people, and second, that his disciples
never repeated their Master's teaching. No doubt what
survives such a brutally crude test must be authentic, but
such a criterion must obviously despair of much else that
is also authentic but happened also, for example, to be of
particular relevance to the first Christians.

However, applying this vastly hostile test to the Gospel narratives, it is interesting to see what happens. It
becomes plain that Jesus is not a manufactured compo-
site of early Christianity in a Jewish context. Jesus does
not disappear from view. For example, often in the
Gospels we find Jesus engaged in controversy with the
rabbis, opposing their traditional Jewish views concerning the Sabbath laws. Yet the matter of Sabbath obser-
vance was not a point of controversy or of great moment
to the early church, and gets hardly any coverage in the
rest of the New Testament. Here is something which fits
the criterion. It is also interesting to realize that concerning the subject of circumcision, which was a great concern to early Christians and almost split the early
church, the Gospels are almost totally silent. In other
words, it really does not look as if the early Christians
were projecting their ideas and their concerns back on to
Jesus in writing the Gospels. Rather it seems that they

were very keen to preserve and report what Jesus actually said and did.

d.   Attention should also be drawn to what is apparently a weakness of the Gospel documents and their accounts of Christ, but which in fact turns out to be a great strength.

When we read the four Gospels it is obvious that they bring to us a basically coherent story of the life and ministry of Jesus. However, on cross-checking the way the same incidents are related in different Gospels we sometimes find details which are not obviously reconcilable. For example, Matthew mentions two demon-possessed men whom Jesus dealt with in the country of the Gadarenes, whereas Mark mentions only one. Or again, the precise chronology of what Jesus did in the last week before his crucifixion shows some apparent differences between Matthew and Mark.

The first thing to say about this kind of thing is that once again we see the artlessness and innocence of the Gospel writers. This is certainly not the mark of people who are setting out to perpetrate a lie. Surely people who are engaged in a conspiracy of lies do their utmost to ensure that there are no easily observable inconsistencies in their stories. Rather these slight differences surely speak of the truth of the event and are the variations which always occur when different people record the same event from different viewpoints.

Secondly, it must be said that on closer inspection, such apparent inconsistencies have frequently been reconciled very convincingly. For example, when the accounts are compared of the first Easter morning, when the resurrection of Christ was discovered, the four Gospels appear to be saying different things. Many people used to say that this showed the utter unreliability of the New Testament. However, after many years of

painstaking study of the New Testament, the geography
of ancient Jerusalem and the relationships between the
various disciples of Jesus and their families, the scholar
John Wenham produced a book which unravelled and
harmonized all the accounts in a most natural and
uncontrived way. Afterwards he wrote, 'It now seems to
me that these resurrection stories exhibit, in a remarkable way, the well-known characteristics of accurate
reporting, for superficially they show great disharmony,
but on close examination the details gradually fall into
place.'[6] Wenham's work argues strongly for the lack of
collusion and yet thorough reliability and precision of
the Gospel writers.

So the quality of the Gospels themselves indicates
that in them we are reading reliable historical accounts.

4. The quality of the witnesses

But why should the accounts of Christ by his first disciples be believed? Not only because, as we have already
seen, their writings show indelible marks of truthfulness,
but also because the writers themselves show qualities of
certainty, honesty and reliability separate from, and
over and above, the documents they wrote.

Firstly, it cannot be denied that these men had obviously experienced a remarkable change. They were
ordinary men, some working in the fishing industry or
tax-collecting. They were men with little or no education
(Acts 4:13). Yet they began a movement which transformed the ancient world and has shaped the course of
history like nothing else. We should listen to them
because they obviously had *something!*

Secondly, they were men who taught and preached
the highest ethical standards of behaviour, and appear to
have lived closely to those standards themselves. They
were not perfect men; they were human. Yet their gospel

would hardly have so gripped the world had they not practised what they preached. They were able, not proudly but humbly, to call other people to follow them as they followed Christ. They were transparently honest men.

Thirdly, they stood for their beliefs in the face of the fiercest hostility of the brutal Roman world. They were prepared to die for what they believed. Some of them, like Peter, were indeed martyred for the gospel's sake. Yet their writings do not come over as those of deluded, rigid fanatics. They come across as the most tender and human of men. There is a quality of character in these witnesses which speaks of the truth of their testimony concerning their Master.

Fourthly, many of these men were from a devout Jewish background, brought up with the highest regard for truthfulness and accuracy.

It should not surprise us, therefore, that such men as these produced such a reliable document as the New Testament. Rather, if we are not going to believe their report we ought to ask ourselves on what grounds we dismiss these men as fools or liars. What right, what evidence, do we have so to impugn their characters?

In this chapter we have seen that if we at least have an open mind on God being real, so that we do not dismiss things out of hand, then there is much to commend Christianity as being historically true. We have seen that the central matters of Christ's story are attested even by the enemies of Christianity. We have seen from considerations of the content of the story itself that it does not look like the kind of story that would have been fabricated. Also we have seen that the New Testament, and the Gospels in particular, come down to us from men of good character and reputation, and that the documents they wrote give every appearance of being truthful and reliable first-hand accounts.

Faced with such evidence many people have felt strongly that the only honest way to refute Christianity is to accept that we do have truthful reports about real events experienced by the disciples of Jesus, but to find some other more credible explanation for them. In particular, since all Christianity either stands or falls by it, they seek an alternative explanation for the resurrection of Jesus.

References

1.   David Kingdon, *Banner of Truth* magazine.
2.   Quoted by Colin Chapman, *The Case for Christianity*, Lion Publications.
3.   As above.
4.   Lord Hailsham, *The Door Wherein I Went*, Collins, 1975, p.33.
5.   Quoted by John Drane, *Introduction to the New Testament*, Lion, p.207.
6.   John Wenham, *Easter Enigma*, Paternoster, 1984.

4.
A better explanation?

It has often been remarked that the resurrection is the keystone of Christianity. If the resurrection of Christ did not happen, then Christianity would tumble. On the other hand, if this most 'incredible' aspect of the gospel story really did occur then we have no reason to reject the rest of it.

Let us think about the resurrection of Christ. Is there a viable alternative which covers the facts?

First of all, this is how the apostle John records the death of Jesus on Good Friday and the initial events of Easter morning: ' . . . Jesus said, "It is finished." With that, he bowed his head and gave up his spirit.

'Now it was the day of Preparation, and the next day was to be a special Sabbath. Because the Jews did not want the bodies left on the crosses during the Sabbath, they asked Pilate to have the legs broken and the bodies taken down. The soldiers therefore came and broke the legs of the first man who had been crucified with Jesus, and then those of the other. But when they came to Jesus and found that he was already dead, they did not break his legs. Instead, one of the soldiers pierced Jesus' side with a spear, bringing a sudden flow of blood and water. The man who saw it has given testimony, and his testimony is true. He knows that he tells the truth. . . Later, Joseph of Arimathea asked Pilate for the body of Jesus

. . . At the place where Jesus was crucified, there was a garden, and in the garden a new tomb, in which no one had ever been laid. Because it was the Jewish day of Preparation and since the tomb was near by, they laid Jesus there.

"Early on the first day of the week, while it was still dark, Mary of Magdala went to the tomb and saw that the stone had been removed from the entrance. So she came running to Simon Peter and the other disciple, the one Jesus loved, and said. "They have taken the Lord out of the tomb, and we don't know where they have put him!"

'So Peter and the other disciple started for the tomb. Both were running, but the other disciple outran Peter and reached the tomb first. He bent over and looked in at the strips of linen lying there but did not go in. Then Simon Peter, who was behind him, arrived and went into the tomb. He saw the strips of linen lying there, as well as the burial cloth that had been around Jesus' head. The cloth was folded up by itself, separate from the linen. Finally the other disciple, who had reached the tomb first, also went inside. He saw and believed. (They still did not understand from Scripture that Jesus had to rise from the dead.)

'Then the disciples went back to their homes, but Mary stood outside the tomb crying. . .' The chapter goes on to tell of the appearances of the risen Lord, first to Mary in the garden, who at first mistook him for the gardener, until he spoke her name, and then to the other disciples.

There are three basic matters which need to be accounted for by any alternative explanation for the resurrection. These are, first the empty tomb, second, the resurrection appearances of Jesus and third the birth and expansion of the Christian church.

Let us consider possible alternative explanations.

1. Jesus did not actually die

To believe this alternative explanation we must believe that, having been scourged with a Roman whip, having hung upon a cross for six hours suspended by nails through his wrists and feet and then having a spear plunged into his side, Jesus could have survived. And not only so, but then within three days Jesus must have been able to give every appearance of being alive from the dead, not as a crippled invalid, but as the risen Lord victorious over death. Is it reasonable to believe that? I don't think it is.

We can propose that Jesus did not really die, but as John reminds us, the fact that Jesus was dead was checked by unbiased people who said he was dead – the Roman soldiers, who no doubt knew their job. They said he was dead (John 19:33). Furthermore, even if somehow they had been mistaken, it was observed that when the spear was thrust into Jesus, 'blood and water' came out, a clear piece of medical evidence that death had occurred (John 19:34).

2. The women mistakenly went to the wrong tomb

The proposal is that in the twilight of the early morning the women made a mistake, found an empty tomb which was the wrong tomb, and the whole idea of Jesus' resurrection just took off from there.

But Mark's Gospel tells us that Mary Magdalene specifically noted where Joseph of Arimathea laid the body of Jesus (Mark 15:47). And if somehow Mary was mistaken, did the other disciples, like Peter and John, also make the same mistake? And if it was all just a mistake, wouldn't the Jewish opponents of Christianity have taken great delight in pointing out the correct tomb? And what about the grave clothes which seem to have been such a factor in leading the apostle John to believe the possibility of the resurrection? (John 20:6-8). Where did they come from, if it was all just a simple mistake? Again, this is proposed as an alternative explanation, but it doesn't appear to hold water.

3. The body of Jesus could have been stolen

But by whom and with what possible motive?

It could have been the Jerusalem authorities, but what motive would they have? The preaching of Jesus' resurrection caused them such trouble later. If they had for some peculiar reason removed it, surely they would have produced it later to quell the rumours spread by the church.

It could have been the disciples. But Matthew tells us that the Jewish authorities set a guard on the tomb specifically in case such a thing was attempted by the disciples, because they knew that Jesus had spoken about his being raised to life after death (Matthew 27:62-66).

It could have been persons unknown for reasons unknown, but that, along with this whole explanation, fails to account for the main thrust of the resurrection accounts, which is not an empty tomb, but the fact that the disciples had met the risen Christ.

In his first letter to the Christians at Corinth, written only just over twenty years after the resurrection, the apostle Paul gives a credal statement of the contents of the preaching of the early Christian church: 'For what I received I passed on to you as of first importance; that Christ died for our sins according to the Scriptures, that he was buried, that he was raised on the third day according to the Scriptures, and that he appeared to Peter, and then to the Twelve. After that he appeared to more than five hundred of the brothers at the same time, most of whom are still living, though some have fallen asleep. Then he appeared to James, then to all the apostles, and last of all he appeared to me also, as to one abnormally born' (1 Corinthians 15:3-8).

This statement by Paul shows that the early preachers spoke primarily not simply about an empty tomb, but about the risen Christ. It shows that the resurrection of Jesus was recognized from the very beginning as a key question for Christianity, because the message of the resurrection of Jesus who had died for our sins was the central truth of the good news. It shows also that the resurrection was preached by Paul as being verified by reliable witnesses, many of whom were still alive and able to be questioned.

4. The appearances of Jesus were just hallucinations

This alternative explanation is that the events of the week in which Jesus was crucified brought tremendous emotional trauma to the disciples, and in the midst of this they had experiences of seeing Jesus which were all in the mind; actually there was nothing there.

However, first, hallucinations do not produce empty graves and grave clothes or roll away enormous stones from rock tombs. If the events of the first Easter were simply hallucinatory, again the enemies of the fledgling church would have produced the body and gleefully dismissed the disciples with a pat on the head as mentally disturbed.

But, secondly, even if we have here a combination of a stolen body and hallucinatory experiences, it is unheard of for 500 people to experience the same hallucination at the same time. A mixed group of people of different personalities normally would not experience the same hallucination, even under the influence of a drug.

However, thirdly, the conversion of the apostle Paul makes such a theory impossible. His conversion to Christ occurred a long time after the initial emotion of the first Easter had died down, when he, a persecutor of Christians and convinced that Christianity was not true, met the risen Lord Jesus Christ as he was on the road to Damascus. Christ was evidently real.

5. The story just got exaggerated

Another theory is that something happened, we cannot be sure what, but it all was simply an exaggeration which snowballed.

But besides missing the point of the obvious honesty of the disciples and the fact of the empty tomb, this simply cannot account for the sudden birth and expansion of the Christian church. The disciples were clearly changed men. They were transformed from being fearful and discouraged into fearless dynamic men who radically changed the world. Mere exaggeration would not account for this. Exaggeration is soon shown for what it is – a lie. These men did not find the strength to turn the world upside down from a frail tissue of lies and exaggeration. A far greater power and certainty than this was manifestly at work.

For 2000 years people have been trying to come up with alternative explanations for the resurrection accounts and nothing even approaching a viable alternative has ever been produced. That is something which speaks for itself.

It is right to remind ourselves also at this point of the work of John Wenham. The Gospel records of the resurrection morning appear to differ. But on close examination they fit together like a beautiful jigsaw puzzle. This is the mark of independent people truthfully recording something which really occurred as they saw it happen.

The resurrection really seems to be a fact which cannot be explained away!

However, seeing the force of the argument for the truth of the resurrection, it is very tempting simply to wish to leave it all in the realm of the unknown, to speak vaguely of the disciples experiencing something unspecified and coming up with a message of redemption for mankind to give vent to their experience and just leave it like that, with a huge question mark.

The German classical historian Erich Stier confronts this. He says, 'Something must really have taken place here; one cannot simply explain it by saying, "The impression which Jesus left behind him in these simple men did not leave them any peace until they thought that they had found the redeeming word for that which they did not understand. Thereby they obtained the power to achieve an unparalleled worldwide effect." It is asking too much to have to believe something like that. That is just not on. I want to state quite categorically that something like that is historically quite out of the question. One cannot just switch off all historical experience in this case, simply because it does not suit us to accept that something very tremendous and great must have taken place here.'[1] It is wrong just to seek to avoid the evidence.

It would appear then that perhaps the simplest explanation for the events of the first Easter is that the Gospel writers were telling the truth. But if the resurrection is true, then there is every reason to believe that all the story of Christ is true.

It is here that the Christian faith stands.

Thinking it over

Has a case been made here for Christianity or not? You should think it over. You may wish to read the last two chapters through again. But we are not to be cowardly and shelve these things. Perhaps for the first time in your life you need to face the fact that Christianity seems to have a tough case, a durable solid foundation in history.

You need to think through also the implications if the historical basis for Christianity is true. First, it must be emphasized that the evidence which we have considered does not just point to cold historical facts and events. It points not only to the truth of certain events, but to much more. The evidence points to the wonderful fact that the God of the universe, the eternal God, has intervened in history on a mission of love. We will think more about this in the next chapter. If the Christian story is true, then God in Christ has reached out to our dying world. If the Christian story is true then God loves men and women and wants them to know him. The evidence concerning Christ is not just fodder for the museum; it speaks of the love of God towards you and me.

But secondly, if the historical basis for Christianity is sound then something else follows. If the story of the resurrection is correct, then although it is true that Jesus lived so long ago, it is also true that he is living now. Although Christianity is rooted in history, it is not stuck in history. It is not just grounded in the past; it is also very much wired into the present. Jesus is alive and can effect our lives for good today. It is this which is the most exciting part. The implication of Christianity being true in history is that it holds out to us a knowledge of the living Lord Jesus Christ through faith in him today.

References

1.   Quoted by Hugo Staudinger, *The Trustworthiness of the Gospels*, Handsel Press, 1981.

5.
Who is Jesus, anyway?

Christianity is calling us to far more than a vague belief in God and in Jesus. It has an urgent message for us. Christianity presents us with a world-view. It claims to present the truth about the world and God, about mankind and its condition. It claims to offer the only true remedy to the ills of our society and of the human soul. It claims to be the greatest good news.

We have looked at some of the evidence concerning Christianity; now we must look at its message. A full explanation of Christianity and all its implications would obviously be a vast undertaking. But the principal components of what Christianity is saying can be summarized in answer to three simple questions: 'Who is Jesus Christ?' 'What is man?' and 'Why did Jesus die on the cross?' In the next three chapters we will consider each of these basic questions in turn.

First, who is Jesus Christ?

Mark begins his Gospel with the words: 'The beginning of the gospel about Jesus Christ, the Son of God' (Mark 1:1). The very essence, the sum and substance of the good news of Christianity, is Jesus Christ. It is the gospel, the good news, about Jesus Christ. John begins his Gospel with the famous words: 'In the beginning was the Word, and the Word was with God, and the Word was God . . . The Word became flesh and made his dwelling among us' (John 1:1,14). He makes it plain that Jesus himself is the Word, Jesus *is* the message, the gospel.

To the church in Rome, a church he had as yet never visited, the apostle Paul introduced himself as 'a servant of Christ Jesus, called to be an apostle and set apart for the gospel of God – the gospel he promised beforehand through his prophets in the Holy Scriptures regarding his Son, who as to his human nature was a descendant of David, and who through the Spirit of holiness was declared with power to be the Son of God, by his resurrection from the dead: Jesus Christ our Lord' (Romans 1:1-4).

Christianity does not preach a mere set of religious rules or a cold philosophy. It preaches a person. It preaches Jesus!

It is worth reflecting a little on what Paul says in those first four verses of Romans. He tells us that the good news centres on the long-promised Messiah of the Old Testament prophets. He has come. He is Jesus Christ, the Son of God.

According to Paul, Jesus is a unique person. He is both human and divine. He is both God and man. As regards his human family tree he is descended from King David, Israel's ancient hero who had rescued the nation from its enemies and established the Jewish people in peace and stability. God had promised David that one of his descendants would be the *eternal* king of God's people (e.g. Psalm 132:11,12; Isaiah 9:6,7). Paul is indicating that Jesus is the one of David's line whom the prophets foretold. You remember how in the Christmas story, Joseph and Mary had to return for tax purposes to register in the town of their ancestors, and they went to Bethlehem, the town of David.

But, of course, the Gospel writers insist that although Jesus was born of Mary as any other child and he was an ordinary baby in that respect, yet his conception was miraculous. Joseph was not his father. Jesus was conceived in Mary's womb by God the Holy Spirit. So it was that the angel told Mary that 'The holy one to be born will be called the Son of God' (Luke 1:35). Thus we find Paul and the other New Testament writers speaking of Jesus both as a man and as the Son of God. Who is Jesus? He is the man who is God, says Christianity.

But on what evidence do Christians base their faith that Jesus is the Son of God? How can we believe that Jesus is God become man? There are four things to say.

The claims of Jesus

1. Firstly, this is not a claim which has been made by the church. *It is something which Jesus certainly claimed for himself.* Christ's remarkable claims can be viewed under three categories: direct claims, implicit claims and what we will call unconscious claims.

Direct claims

Looking at the Gospels, we find that Jesus spoke a great deal about himself. In this he was very different from the religious teachers of his day and in fact from all other great religious leaders. It has often been rightly said that the message of the other major religions can be summarized as, 'That is the truth, follow that,' whereas Jesus spoke in terms of 'I am the truth, follow me.'

He claimed to be the bread which alone could give life, the light which alone could dispel the world's darkness and the only door of salvation (John 6:35; 8:12; 10:9; 14:6). These claims are startling, but all the more so because they each begin by emphasizing 'I am. . .' and to the Jews '*I am*' was one of the great names of God himself. When God called Moses, back in Israel's past, to return to Egypt to lead his people out of slavery at the Exodus, Moses asked God, 'Who shall I say sent me?'

God's reply was 'I am who I am. This is what you are to say to the Israelites: "I AM has sent me to you"' (Exodus 3:14). It was clear to the Jews that Jesus was claiming to be equal with God (John 5:18); that was why on a number of occasions the Jews tried to stone Jesus, thinking he was uttering blasphemy. We read in John's Gospel, 'Again the Jews picked up stones to stone him, but Jesus said to them, "I have shown you many great miracles from the Father. For which of these do you stone me?" "We are not stoning you for any of these," replied the Jews, "but for blasphemy, because you, a mere man, claim to be God"'(John 10:31-33; cf 8:58-59).

Jesus claimed to be the Messiah promised for centuries by the Old Testament (Mark 8:29). He asserted that Abraham, who lived around 2000 BC, had seen him, and that Moses, whose date is about 1500 BC, wrote of him and, indeed, that all the Old Testament pointed to him (John 8:56, 5:46; Luke 24:27). He declared that man's principal duty was to believe on him (John 6:29), and that not to do so was the greatest sin (John 3:19). He claimed always to please God the Father (John 8:29). If anyone loved anything or anybody more than Jesus, he was not worthy of him. Not even a person's family may come first (Matthew 10:37-39). And it was to himself that he invited those who heard him to come (Matthew 11:28-30).

Yet these astonishing claims were not the claims of a megalomaniac, for when people wanted to make Jesus king after he had performed one of his most lovely miracles in feeding the 5000, he withdrew himself and hid from the crowds (John 6:15). It was not popularity and power that Jesus was after. But coolly and calmly he claimed to be the Son of God, the Way, the Truth and the Life.

Implicit claims

Often we meet situations in the Gospels where the

actions and words of Jesus indirectly make it plain that he knew himself to be God.

Take, for example, a striking incident in Mark's Gospel, chapter 2. Jesus was speaking to a large crowd inside a house. A paralysed man, carried by four friends, was being brought to Jesus hoping to be healed, but the house was so crowded that they could not get in. In order to reach Jesus they climbed up on the roof and took off the tiles and lowered him through to Jesus! I do not know what the house owner thought! However, since entering a house this way was a common technique of burglars in those days, it is possible that the cripple and his friends were criminals, and perhaps the man had even received his injury in a burglary. But, whether or not that speculation is true, Jesus, seeing the faith of these men, immediately reacted on seeing the man lowered down to him by saying, 'Son, your sins are forgiven' (Mark 2:5).

Now, when we think about it, that is quite an extraordinary thing to say. Just suppose these men were burglars and they had burgled your house and stolen your money, and Jesus said, 'I forgive them.' Your first reaction might well have been to think, 'Who does he think he is? What impertinence! It was not his money they stole, but mine! If there is any forgiving to do it is for me to forgive, not him!' But, you see, Jesus here is assuming himself to be God, against whom all sins are committed, and who alone has the right ultimately to forgive sins. Here is an implicit claim that he is God.

Some Pharisees who happened to be there at the time understood this and thought to themselves, 'Why does this fellow talk like that? He's blaspheming! Who can forgive sins but God alone?' And Jesus, knowing their thoughts, responded, 'Which is easier; to say to the paralytic, "Your sins are forgiven", or to say, "Get up, take your mat and walk"? But that you may know that the Son of Man has authority on earth to forgive sins

. . ." He said to the paralytic, "I tell you, get up, take your mat and go home."' And it happened! The man was healed and got up and walked out in full view of them all.

This implicit understanding of himself as God the Son is often very obvious as we compare the way Jesus performed his miracles with the miracles performed by the men of the Old Testament, or with those of the apostles later on after Jesus' ministry. These men used to perform miracles as they prayed and called on God's name. By contrast, Jesus healed in his own name, not calling upon or praying to God. Here is just one example: 'A man with leprosy came and knelt before him and said, "Lord, if you are willing, you can make me clean." Jesus reached out his hand and touched the man. "I am willing," he said, "Be clean!" Immediately he was cured of his leprosy' (Matthew 8:2,3). Who but God himself could handle the situation that way?

A week after the resurrection, according to John's Gospel, doubting Thomas met the risen Lord Jesus Christ. His doubts disintegrated and he worshipped Jesus, calling him 'my Lord and my God' (John 20:28). And Jesus accepted that worship. What is the implication? Lord and God is what he claims to be!

3. Unconscious claims

It is very often the things which we say or do when we are not aware of ourselves, the little asides and off-the-cuff remarks, which reveal our true selves. There is a story I once heard from an old friend who was a university mathematics lecturer. I do not know how true it was, but it illustrates the point very well. It concerned two young men doing their final exams. One was very bright and the other an average student. The average lad had got a view of the other fellow's answers and thought he would do some cheating and copy. But there was a question on the paper which had been misprinted and did not make sense. The bright young man wrote on his answer paper, 'I have read this question, and I cannot answer it because I do not think it makes sense.' The other lad copied him, but unfortunately he wrote, 'I have read this question and I cannot answer it because I do not think it makes sense *either*.' That one unconscious word said it all! The cat was out of the bag!

The things we say when we are not thinking of ourselves give so much away. But even the asides of Jesus, the seemingly unconscious remarks of Christ, bear the marks of his knowing himself to be the Son of God. It was not a claim which he relaxed or forgot about when he thought other people were not looking or when he was not thinking of himself. One incident in particular stands out. On one occasion Jesus was thinking of Jerusalem and he began to become deeply emotional, lamenting tenderly for the city and its sins and the lost people there. He said, 'O Jerusalem, Jerusalem, you who kill the prophets and stone those sent to you, how often I have longed to gather your children together, as a hen gathers her chicks under her wings, but you were not willing!' (Luke 13:34). He is not thinking of himself and yet quite suddenly he is claiming to be the one who through all the centuries has looked down on Israel, the one to whom the gathering of the people should be, the one who in his love for the Jews has sent the prophets and leaders. He is claiming to be God in that tender, emotional, 'unconscious' moment.

So it can be seen that at every level Jesus asserted that he was none other than God incarnate. Christianity's claim that Jesus is the Son of God is not something which the church or any of the early Christians has dreamed up. It is something the church has always believed, firstly because this is who Jesus claimed to be.

The testimony of the eyewitnesses

2. But secondly, Christianity proclaims Jesus as God incarnate because *this is how his first disciples came to understand him.*

The disciples lived with Jesus for three years, all day, every day. They heard his claims. They talked with him, travelled with him, they got up in the morning with him. They washed with him and ate with him. Others saw Jesus only in his public moments, but they had the opportunity to observe him all the time. They saw him joyful, pressurized, tired, hungry, sad even to death. But remarkably their familiarity never bred even a shadow of contempt. Rather it brought a deepening conviction that they were witnessing the most remarkable life ever lived.

They make it plain in their writings that even though they had seen him under extreme tiredness with people mocking and scorning him and seeking to provoke him by their unfair and untrue accusations – all the kinds of things which would normally lead us to lose our self-control – they never saw any sign of sin in him (1 Peter 1:19; 2:22; 1 John 3:5; cf. 2 Corinthians 5:21; Hebrews 7:26).

Again, the first disciples call Jesus 'God'. Matthew speaks plainly of the infant Jesus as 'God with us' (Matthew 1:23). This witness of the disciples concerning Jesus should carry great weight with us, not only because they were contemporaries of Jesus but especially because of their Jewish background.

All the first disciples were orthodox Jews. All had been brought up to believe that God is *one* and there is no other. The Christian doctrine of the Trinity, that God is one and yet three at the same time, is not something which a religious Jew can easily come to accept. And yet as they saw the life of Jesus, as they saw that Jesus claimed to be God himself and at the same time he would pray to God the Father in heaven, they could not come to any other conclusion. The evidence which confronted them was too great. They came to believe that Jesus was God the Son become man, and they were prepared to stake their lives on it. We should take that witness seriously.

The only explanation that makes sense

3. Then, thirdly, Christians believe that Jesus is God become man because *there is no other way for us to make sense of what we know of Jesus*. In fact the whole behaviour and teaching of Jesus in the four Gospels is inexplicable if he was not the Son of God.

There is a very famous quotation from C.S. Lewis which sums up the logic of this magnificently. Lewis says, 'I am trying here to prevent anyone from saying the really foolish thing that people often say about him, "I am ready to accept Jesus as a great moral teacher, but I don't accept his claim to be God." This is the one thing we must not say. A man who was merely a man and said the sort of things that Jesus said would *not* be a great moral teacher. He would either be a lunatic – on the level of a man who says he is a poached egg – or else he would be the devil from hell. You must take your choice. Either this man was and is the Son of God; or else a madman or something worse. You can shut him up as a fool, you can spit at him and kill him as a demon; or you can fall at his feet and call him Lord and God. But let us not come with any patronizing nonsense about his being a great moral teacher. He has not left that open to us. He did not intend to.'[1] Was Jesus really mad? Or a demon? No. Then he must be who he claimed to be – the Son of God.

The evidence of the resurrection

4. But, fourthly, on top of these solid reasons comes the great fact of *the resurrection*. All men are born and die, and that is the end of them. But God has marked out the man Jesus in the most unmistakable way as being unlike any other man. God raised him from the dead never to die again.

How do we know that Jesus is the Son of God? Because God raised him from the dead. In the words of St Paul at the beginning of Romans, the evidence that Christ is God is that he 'was declared with power to be the Son of God by his resurrection from the dead'.

Jesus taught many things and claimed many things during his life, including calling himself the Son of God. If all his claims had been mere words then when Jesus died on the cross that would have been the last anyone would have heard of him. But, as we have already seen in chapter 4, a great weight of evidence suggests that Jesus did not stay dead. He was raised back to life again. And his resurrection was God's vindication of his Son. By the resurrection, in unmistakable terms, God declared that Jesus was no impostor, but that he was precisely who he claimed to be.

Here then is the first major component of the Christian gospel. It proclaims that Jesus Christ is God become man. When Jesus was born in Bethlehem, in that out-of-the-way little town in Palestine, something truly stupendous was occurring – God was entering the history of the world. This is the beginning of the good news for us all.

But obviously we are caused to ask 'Why?' For what reason did God become man? This brings us to our second question, which introduces us to the message of Christianity, 'What is man?'

References

1.   C. S. Lewis, *Mere Christianity*, Fontana, 1955, p.52.

6.
People – God's lost treasure

Christianity not only speaks of Christ; it also presents us with a diagnosis of the human condition. Perhaps the most obvious observation of all as we look at our world is that things are not right. There always seems to be so much tragedy and terror in our newspapers and on the TV screen. I can actually remember a magazine article not long ago entitled 'How to survive the evening news'. How tragic! Our world is a bit of a mess, to say the least, and by and large our world is what we have made it. Yes, there are natural disasters, but more often we read of disasters in which the hand of man has played a large part. It has been well said that Christianity's analysis of our situation is that the nature of the human condition is the condition of human nature. Why did Christ come? Simply because something has gone terribly wrong with humanity. Something is desperately wrong with man. There needed to be a rescue. Let us see in more detail what Christianity says about people and what is wrong with us. Again we can summarize things under four headings.

1. Man – the image of God

Confronted with some of mankind's faults and failings,

some people say, 'Well, you can't really expect consistent higher behaviour from man, for after all, man is just an animal. He is the highest form of animal, but he is just an animal for all that, and so you must not be surprised if he often behaves like one. You must not be surprised, for example, at man's inhumanity to man.'

This is an approach to the question 'What is man?' which is based upon a world-view which has rejected God. The popular idea of the theory of evolution suggests that all life began by chance and that man has developed from the apes. This obviously provides the background to the idea that people are the highest form of animal, but are still animals nevertheless. During the 1960s this whole approach was popularized in Britain by Dr Desmond Morris, with his comparisons between animal behaviour and human behaviour published in his famous paperback *The Naked Ape*.

This answer to our question clearly contains much that is true. Physically, anatomically and environmentally we *do* share much in common with the animals. But even looking at the idea on its own terms, of having erased God from the picture at the outset, there seem to be great inadequacies in this view which indicate that it does not actually give us a true view of man.

Firstly, *man's achievements, culturally and scientifically, are on such a different scale to that of the animals* that the idea of man and animals being fundamentally the same is called into question. Beavers may build dams, but men develop quantum mechanics and computers, paint the Mona Lisa and fly to the moon! To say that animals and man are the same is like saying that coal and diamonds are the same. They are, yet they aren't, are they? There is something essentially different.

Secondly, other animals (if that is what we are) appear perfectly contented with warmth, food, shelter, exercise, health and the companionship of their own kind. When their basic needs are met the animals seem to be perfectly happy creatures. But that is not how it is with mankind. *There is something in man which yearns to reach beyond this present world.* People are somehow too big for what the world can provide. This manifests itself in various ways. It is seen in mankind's almost universal pursuit of some kind of religion. We seem to need to try to touch the eternal. It is seen in the popularity of what we call 'fantasy' literature, novels which take the reader into other worlds, or into another time where things are very different from this world. It is seen in our unique ability to appreciate what we call 'art' and 'beauty'. It shows itself in the life and death of a man like Ernest Hemingway. Hemingway was a tremendously successful novelist and in life 'had it all'. From wine, women and song, to bullfights in Spain and big game hunts in Africa, Hemingway pursued all that this world had to offer to the full. And yet he never found satisfaction in life. As a man in his sixties he eventually committed suicide, blowing his brains out and leaving a suicide note stating that 'Life is just one damn thing after another.' If man is just an animal, why do we long for more than this world can give? No, it seems there is something 'spiritual' about us. We share much with the animals but we do not really fit into the same slot. To be human, and to describe what it is to be human, requires categories which are beyond the animal and unique to ourselves.

But thirdly, although there is a sense in which we are elevated way above the animal world, many people would say with some justification that there is a sense in which man can be 'worse than an animal', and that in itself can point to our being something other than the animals. When we speak like this we may be thinking of certain heinous crimes of man, or man's pollution and destruction of the environment. An animal acts by instinct, not 'knowing' what it is doing. Yet intelligent people can *knowingly* act in the most callous, perverted

or destructive way. Our own land is the land where the
Moors Murders were committed. Our own century is the
century of the Nazi concentration camps and of the
labour camps and 'psychiatric' hospitals in the USSR, of
indiscriminate terrorism, and the stark denial of basic
human rights in South Africa. This is something 'other'
than the animal.

Indeed at the less serious level of the more common
human misdemeanours people take a delight in actually
knowing that what is being done is 'naughty' or 'wrong'.
'Go on be a devil, enjoy yourself' people say. That is
something which would never occur to an animal and it
indicates that there is something 'godlike' (god with a
small 'g') about us even in our evils.*

It is for reasons such as these that although the *Naked
Ape* view of man may be interesting, it is in my estimation inadequate, and it is for the same reasons that the
biblical view of man commends itself.

In the opening chapters of Genesis, where the Bible
explains about the beginnings of our world, it speaks of
the animals being created by God 'each according to
their kinds' (Genesis 1:21,24,25). But when it speaks of
the creation of man and woman a strikingly different
phrase is used. God says, 'Let us make man *in our image*,
in our likeness' (Genesis 1:26). And then, as if to re-
emphasize the uniqueness of human beings, the next
verse reads, 'So God created man in his own image, in
the image of God he created him; male and female he
created them' (Genesis 1:27). Whereas the animals were
created according to various patterns in God's mind, for
human beings God himself is the pattern. This makes
human beings different from the animals and bestows
upon us a vast dignity.

In particular, though man shares a similar chemistry
and biology to the animals, being made out of the same
earth, yet unlike the animals, man is a spiritual being. Of
man alone do we read that God himself 'breathed into

his nostrils the breath of life, and the man became a living being' (Genesis 2:7).

Men and women are spiritual creatures. They were made for friendship and fellowship with God. That is why the things of this material world can never bring total satisfaction in life. We were made by God and for God and, as the great theologian St Augustine of Hippo put it, 'Our hearts are restless until they find their rest in God.' Men and women, boys and girls are creatures of the greatest value and dignity. We were made in the image of God himself. We were made to know God.

There is a lovely passage in the *Meditations* of the English poet John Donne which captures the dignity of human beings and the fact that we are in a sense greater than the world we live in: 'Man consists of more pieces, more parts, than the world; than the world doeth, nay than the world is. And if those pieces were extended, and stretched out in man as they are in the world, man would be the giant and the world the dwarf; the world but the map and the man the world. If all the veins in our bodies were extended to be rivers, and all the sinews to mines, and all the muscles that lie upon one another to hills, and all the bones to quarries of stones and all the pieces to the proportion of those which correspond to them in the world, the air would be too little for this Orb of Man to move in, the firmament would be but enough for this star; for as the whole earth hath nothing to which something in man doth not answer, so hath man many pieces, of which the whole world hath no representation . . . Our creatures are our thoughts, creatures that are born giants; that reach from East to West, from earth to heaven, that do not only bestride the sea and land but span the Sun and firmament at once. My thoughts reach all, comprehend all. Inexplicable mystery; I their Creator am in a close prison, in a sick bed, anywhere, and any one of my creatures, my thoughts, is with the Sun, and beyond the Sun, and overtakes the Sun and

overgoes the Sun in one pace, one step, anywhere.'
Human beings are made in God's image.

The next thing we must see about man concerns his
moral nature.

2. Man – under the law

What was the first thing you learned to say when you
were a baby? I don't suppose you can remember. But did
your parents ever tell you later? Suppose we made a list,
starting with the first word we spoke, then the second,
then the third etc.; it would be quite an interesting list.
Maybe something like 'Dadda' or 'Mummy' would be at
the top, and 'dog' or 'book' second. And I would guess
that not right at the top of that list, but not too far down
the list would come the words 'It's not fair!' I can
remember saying those words as a little child. Our own
children have uttered the same immortal phrase from
earliest days! And I guess that they are words which
come early and readily to us all.

The second thing we have to say about man is that not
only do we have a spiritual side to our nature, but *we also
are moral creatures*. We have a great sense of right and
wrong – especially when it concerns ourselves! From
earliest days through to our old age we make judgements
concerning situations, other people and even sometimes
ourselves. We say, 'She's right!' or 'That's wrong!'

No matter how sceptical some people might be about
morality in theory, as soon as a moral issue enters our
own lives – we are attacked, or robbed, or swindled etc.
– we find ourselves making judgements about rightness
and wrongness. Whether we call it conscience, or whatever, we all seem to have an in-built sense of morality.

The question is, where does it come from? That is a
question which, as we saw in chapter 2, is particularly
difficult to answer if we discount God and believe that

we and our world came about by chance. How can you get right and wrong out of blind chance? Here are some ways people argue.

Some people try to argue that morality is just about trying to produce *the greatest good for the greatest number* of people. That is a very fine aim, but actually it will not provide a basis for right and wrong. In fact, the idea of the greatest good for the greatest number can be manipulated to justify almost anything, including the greatest evils. For example, a widely used school mathematics text book used in Nazi Germany before World War II was *Mathematics in the Service of Political Education*. One edition includes problems stated in rather distorted terms of the cost of caring for and rehabilitating the chronically sick and crippled. One of the problems asked in this book, for instance, is how many new housing units could be built and how many marriage-allowance loans could be given to newly-wed couples for the amount of money it cost the state to care for 'the crippled and the insane'.[1] It was that kind of thinking which paved the way for the holocaust and the concentration camps. 'Get rid of the unwanted human refuse who are such a drain on society, so it can be better for the rest of us!'

The idea of the greatest good for the greatest number is a fine idea, but once it is cut adrift as the lone definition of morality, it can easily become mere economics and be used to justify the most terrible immorality which offends our inbuilt sense of right and wrong.

Other people argue that right and wrong are just a matter of *personal opinion*. There are no absolutes in morality. There is just the way you see things and the way I see things. There is only personal ethics. You decide what is right for you, and I decide what is right for me, but I must not try to impose my ideas on you, and you must not try to impose your ethics on me. On the surface this would seem to be a very civilized and

sensible way of carrying on. But the problem is that our
sense of right and wrong goes far deeper than that.
People can say, 'Morality is just your opinion against
mine,' but that is not how they react when they read of
child abuse, or terrorism, or of a confidence trickster
who fiddles old age pensioners out of their money. We
don't say, 'That's just his opinion, his way of behaving.'
We say with all our moral indignation 'That's wrong!' If
morality is just a matter of personal opinion then we
have no basis for a legal system. You can't send people
to prison over differences in personal opinion.

Again, you see, our inbuilt sense of morality is something more strident and real than personal opinion
would allow it to be. When people understand this, their
reaction is to say, 'Well, we have to have law to protect
society,' (which is right and proper) and then they have
to fall back on to the argument about the greatest good
for the greatest number to find a basis for it. But as we
have seen already, this explanation will not do either.

'Our sense of right and wrong is just some instinct of
self-preservation left over from our evolutionary past,'
say some people. But again that does not fit the bill.
Morality is not just a matter of self-preservation, for we
exercise moral judgements quite often in things which
are of no direct concern to our personal preservation.
We even get morally outraged about cricket umpires and
football referees! And, besides, we try to overcome
other instincts related to self-preservation – such as the
fear of falling – when they get in the way of what we want
to do. But our attitude to the rapist or the drug trafficker
who is destroying the lives of young people is not
'There's someone who has managed to overcome
instincts to which sadly I am still captive.' We say, 'No!
This is terribly wrong!'

Morality is something which cannot be explained
away. Whether we like it or not, we are moral creatures

and we live in a moral world. Society would collapse without law and order, and each one of us has an inherent sense of right and wrong somehow written into us.

Why is this? The only answer that makes sense is that we are living not in a world which has come about by chance, but in God's world. The Bible says that we are moral creatures made in God's image, and answerable to him for the way we live our lives.

God's own character is the fundamental basis for what is right and just. He is the holy God who is the foundation of all creation. His character is what is right and good, and all that offends against the holy character of God is therefore wrong, and wrong in the most absolute sense.

God's law, which we will discuss in more detail in the next section, reflects his character, and because we are made in his image something of this holy law of God is written in our hearts and witnesses to the fact that we are accountable to him.

Many people would like to think that the world happened at random, that the universe is a 'free lunch', and that therefore life is fundamentally amoral. But the very way we live belies this idea. We live in God's world under God's law. We make moral judgements all the time. In this letter to the Romans the apostle Paul comments on the moral sense of people who have never had or seen a Bible. He writes, 'When Gentiles, who do not have the law, do by nature things required by the law, they are a law for themselves, even though they do not have the law, since they show that the requirements of the law are written on their hearts, their consciences also bearing witness, and their thoughts now accusing, now even defending them' (Romans 2:14-15). Moral awareness is inbuilt in mankind.

First we saw that biblical Christianity teaches that human beings have the immense dignity of originally being made in the image of God. But secondly we have seen that this means that man is also a being who is morally aware and accountable to God his Maker.

3. Man – the inveterate rebel

The nineteenth-century French poet and art historian Charles Baudelaire had a famous sentence: 'If there is a God, he is the devil.' What Baudelaire was saying was that if God created our world, as we see it with all its tragedy and pain, then he is an evil god.[2] And not only so, but something else follows. If God made the world with all its disease and death, its poverty and injustice, then these are things that are 'right' and to fight against them is to fight against God.

Clearly Jesus did not go along with that. He wept over death. He healed disease and claimed to be serving God at the same time. He cared for the oppressed. How could he do that?

Indeed if the world as it is now is the way God originally created it, then such actions would be to resist God. But clearly Christ and Christianity teach that the present world is very different from the way it was created originally. A great discontinuity has occurred in the history of our world. A profound tragedy has taken place, which has brought into this world things which are evil and which God never placed here in the beginning. So to resist these things is not to resist God, but rather to work with God.

The great upset which changed the course of our history so drastically is the Fall of man. The first human beings, the pinnacle of God's creation, made in his image to be his vice-regents upon earth, rebelled against God. This rebellion against God is called sin. Adam, the first man, fell into sin and his life and the world were disrupted in the most immense and tragic way. Evil entered (Genesis 3:1-7; Romans 5:12-14).

Our natural tendencies to sympathize with one another as human beings would encourage us to find some mitigating circumstance, some hidden though noble motive behind what our first parents did. 'Surely God was oppressive in his handling of them, and they were reaching for freedom. Surely God was denying them the fulfilment of all their potential and capabilities and they had to aspire to a greater maturity.' But according to the Bible this was not the case.

Then what was the motive behind their rebellion? It was that they desired to be as God. It was that they wished to usurp the position of God. This is the essence of all sin. It is to rebel against God and our obligations to him, and to, as it were, make ourselves God. This was the great and damning evil, that the creature should seek to dethrone the benevolent Creator, who had bestowed upon him nothing but good, and to whom he owed literally everything. According to Christianity, it was man's rebellion against God that ruined the world.

We need to see four things about the Christian doctrine of sin.

1. As a result of the Fall, all people have become sinners. We all probably know the colloquialism, 'Like father, like son'. When we use this phrase we are speaking about a father and son having the same kind of physical features or personalities. Christianity teaches that somehow, as Adam, the father and head of the whole human race, fell into sin, so all we his children have inherited the same character. We are rebels against God. We too are sinners (Romans 3:10,11,23).

By saying that we are all sinners, Christianity is not saying that people are all as thoroughly bad as they possibly could be. You do not have to be profligate to be a sinner. The core of sin is the rebellious heart. Perhaps outwardly some people are very respectable and civil. They do not swear, they do not steal other men's wives, or other women's husbands. But nevertheless inside there is a heart which wishes to live without God. Inside there is a heart which rejects God's authority over their lives and says, 'It's *my* life. God will not rule over me, I will live life *my* way.' That is the essence of sin and it is in us all.

One of the more ugly and unhelpful faces of religion is the 'holier-than-thou' attitude of some religious people. But anyone who adopts such an attitude, and so looks down on others, is wrong and has misunderstood the very beginning of Christianity's diagnosis of mankind. The message of the Bible tells us that no man or woman has the right to look down upon his or her neighbour. Perhaps some people's sins are more obvious than others, but we are all in the same boat. We are all sinners. (And for that reason we ought to look compassionately on one another.) We are all rebels against God.

2.   But why should we believe this story about Adam and his rebellion against God? 'Surely it's just a myth,' some people would say. Can we really believe that this actually took place in the history of our world?

Certainly, the story of the temptation of Adam and Eve in Eden finds a ready echo in the experience of mankind, and in that sense it is a 'mythical' story – in the sense that it is a story with a meaning for us all.

The nature of Adam and Eve's sin finds a very close replica in the outlook on life so prevalent among mankind. They wanted to be like God. They desired to be independent, all-powerful and invulnerable. And isn't the ultimate goal of modern materialistic greed precisely the same? Not just to have enough, but to have power. Not just to be secure, but to be invulnerable with no need for God. Again, God in Eden was the centre of the world. But our first parents desired that position, and fallen man today puts self, instead of God, at the centre of his world. In the sense of having a constant meaning for us, the story of the Fall in Eden is mythical.†

But there are reasons to believe that it is *not* mythical

in any other sense. The Bible teaches that the story of Adam and Eve actually happened. It is actually true and this explains some of both the genetic and behavioural aspects of man today.

Firstly, modern genetics has shown that the idea of the whole human race being descended from one human pair is not such a fanciful one as some people have made it out to be. There are all kinds of different people in the world, fat and thin, black and white and yellow, tall and short etc. But scientists now tell us that despite all the superficial differences, all people alive today are actually genetically very similar. In fact there is likely to be more difference between two white folk taken at random, than between, say, the average white person and the average Chinese or average Nigerian. And these similarities are so great that biologists are beginning to propose that all human beings are descended from one woman. So the idea of Adam and Eve is not so incredible.[3]

Secondly, why should we take the idea of man's original rebellion so seriously? Well, because of a very simple observation concerning mankind. We all recognize morality and yet we all fail to live up to it. We all have a good idea of what is right and yet any honest person would own the fact that 'No one is perfect', including himself. But if morality is something which comes naturally to us, why do we fail to live up to it? On the other hand, if we really are basically the same as the animals, why do we have a sense of morality in the first place, why do we ever feel guilty? No, the fact of man's moral awareness and yet his confessed inability to live up even to his own moral standards demands some kind of disruption or discontinuity in the development of mankind. It results from the Fall. The inner contradiction of man the moralist and man the moral failure indicates that man is not now what he was originally. Only the idea of a God who is the source of moral order, and a human

race estranged from that God, explains mankind. The
biblical story of the Fall makes sense, and I would
suggest *alone* makes sense.
3.   No one likes to be called a sinner, but the fact that
we are sinners is revealed to us as we look at our lives in
the light of the standards of the Bible.

God's law, the Ten Commandments, runs as follows.
God says to us, 'You shall have no other gods (objects of
worship) before me. You shall not make for yourself an
idol (man cannot *make* the true God). You shall not
misuse the name of the Lord your God. Remember to
keep one day in seven as a day of rest, set apart for God.
Honour your father and your mother. You shall not
murder. You shall not commit adultery. You shall not
steal. You shall not tell lies. You shall not covet things
which do not belong to you.'

In our consciences we know all this to be perfectly
right. Our inbuilt sense of morality, which we spoke of
earlier, affirms this law. And yet there is not one of us
who has always kept this law. Look, for example, at the
last command. Have we never been envious of other
people's goods? The law reveals us to be sinners, rebels
against God and his commands.

This becomes especially clear as Jesus later explained
that the law of God not only applies to our outward
actions, but even to our inner thoughts. For example, he
said, 'You have heard that it was said, "Do not commit
adultery." But I tell you that anyone who looks at a
woman lustfully has already committed adultery with
her in his heart"' (Matthew 5:27-28). As we read this, we
are exposed as sinners in the sight of a holy God.

Again, the apostle Paul sets before us some lovely
instructions in his letters concerning how human life is to
be conducted. Here is one such passage: 'But the fruit of
the Spirit is love, joy, peace, patience, kindness, good-
ness, faithfulness, gentleness and self-control. Against

such things there is no law' (Galatians 5:22,23). Here is
another: 'Love is patient, love is kind. It does not envy,
it does not boast, it is not proud. It is not rude, it is not
self-seeking, it is not easily angered, it keeps no record
of wrongs. Love does not delight in evil but rejoices with
the truth. It always protects, always trusts, always
hopes, always perseveres' (1 Corinthians 13:4-7). A
beautiful pattern and quality of life is set out for us in
passages like these. We *know* this is how we should live
and perhaps we would even aspire to live like this. But
we would all have to agree that often we fall tremendously far short of these standards. We are revealed to be
sinners. It is as the Bible states. We are moral beings, but
moral failures in the sight of a holy God. This is the root
of mankind's problems and it is our greatest problem
personally. We are made by God, in the image of God,
for friendship with God. But we are separated from God
because of our sin. We are culpable and we are guilty.

4.   But perhaps the most tragic feature of man's fall into
sin is that sin has not left man as it found him. It has dam-
aged mankind. It has levied a terrible toll. Sin has done
two things to man: it has blinded him, and it has brought
him into bondage.

Firstly, it has destroyed people's natural ability to
perceive God, or respond to God. It has made us as
insensitive to God, by nature, as a blind man is to the
world around him. The apostle Paul puts it like this: as
Adam and Eve rejected God, 'their thinking became
futile and their foolish hearts were darkened. Although
they claimed to be wise they became fools . . .' (Romans
1:21-22), and we have inherited this same blindness. We
are just like our first parents. We are innately willing
rebels against God and at the same time blind to God.

So the situation is complex. Man's rebellion against
God has left him in the worst possible position. He is
both culpable and incapable. How can you hold a blind

man responsible for the things he cannot do, as he can't
see? Those two things may seem irreconcilable. They
are in the physical world, but not in the spiritual world.
Let me put it to you like this from my own experience.
Before I became a Christian I was aware of two things. I
was aware that in all honesty I could say that I was not
sure about God. I was incapable of perceiving him. I was
blind. But I also knew that even if somebody could suddenly make Christ appear to me in a blaze of light so that
I could be absolutely certain of him, there was something in me which still would not want to surrender to
him. I was an inveterate rebel. So I was blind and
culpable at the same time. This is something of the complex web into which man has fallen by his rejection of
God.

But secondly, sin has brought man into bondage. Sin
has, as it were, an addictive effect. We have been
brought into a state in which things which displease God
are things which we enjoy and which we therefore naturally choose. Whether this finds expression in the more
gross sins of the promiscuous society, or simply in the
civil self-centredness of the respectable middle classes,
the root is the same. It is the slavery which Martin
Luther called 'the heart turned in upon itself'.

The apostle Paul sums it up like this: 'The mind of sinful man is death . . . the sinful mind is hostile to God. It
does not submit to God's law, nor can it do so. Those
controlled by the sinful nature cannot please God'
(Romans 8:6-8).

So the Christian diagnosis of man spells out that man,
with the immense dignity of being made in the image of
God, is morally responsible before the holy God, but has
rebelled against God and his commands, and has fallen
into a state in which this rebellion has become natural to
him.

4. Man – under God's judgement

The wrath of God is something which it seems people do not like to mention much today, because they prefer to dwell on his love. We can all understand that. But Bible Christianity would say that we will never understand the world or the gospel of Jesus Christ and the real meaning of the love of God unless we are also prepared to understand God's anger. The apostle Paul begins to explain the gospel in his letter to the church in Rome by starting just here. He says, 'The wrath of God is being revealed from heaven against all the godlessness and wickedness of men who suppress the truth by their wickedness . . .' (Romans 1:18).

The anger of God is not a popular concept, but here is an incident which might help us to understand it.

Not long ago as a family we were visiting friends in the north of England. It was a lovely sunny summer's day and soon after we arrived and had unpacked the car the boys of the two families, aged about ten and eleven, went off to the local park with their equipment to play cricket.

They had not been there long when a gang of older lads came by, and when our boys would not let them join in, things got rough. Our youngest boy was attacked by two teenagers and was kicked and punched; he came running back to the house in tears with mud and boot marks all over his shirt.

Now, I think you will understand that when this happened I felt very, very angry. I felt that if I could have got hold of those older lads at that moment I would have given them what for! I felt wrath!

Christianity speaks of the anger of God, and the first thing it tells us is that God is not angry for nothing. He has been provoked to wrath, just as I was provoked by the attack on my boy. God is provoked by human sin. 'The wrath of God is being revealed . . . against all godlessness and wickedness . . .' Wrath is the holy God's reaction to sin. Just as I was angry about how my son was treated, so when God sees the way people abuse his laws and one another, he is angry.

My wrath, no doubt, had much that was unhelpful and sinful mixed up with it. I don't have the right to judge other people as God does. My anger would probably have been expressed as uncontrolled vengeance; I was so very angry. But God's wrath is not like that. Although there is passion in it, it is a *holy* passion, a just expression of anger.

And my wrath was never expressed (mainly because the wife of the home where we were staying had telephoned the police and I felt it was therefore best to keep out of it, or I might have been arrested too!). But God's anger does find expression. It is, in the words of Paul, 'being revealed'.

How is the wrath of God expressed? Having spoken of the wrath of God, the apostle Paul in the first two chapters of his letter to the Romans mentions two ways in which this wrath is unleashed.

1. The first thing which Paul says about the outworking of God's wrath pertains to the present, the here and now, and perhaps it is not what we would have expected. It is simply that *God lets people go their own way*. God does not seek to restrain people from the sin that they have chosen. Three times in the first chapter of Romans comes the terrible phrase 'God gave them over'.

'Therefore *God gave them over* in the sinful desires of their hearts to sexual impurity for the degrading of their bodies with one another. They exchanged the truth of God for a lie, and worshipped and served created things rather than the Creator – who is for ever praised. Amen.

'Because of this, *God gave them over* to shameful lusts. Even their women exchanged natural relations for unnatural ones. In the same way the men also abandoned natural relations with women and were inflamed with lust for one another. Men committed indecent acts with other men, and received in themselves the due penalty for their perversion.

'Furthermore, since they did not think it worth while to retain the knowledge of God, *he gave them over* to a depraved mind, to do what ought not to be done. They have become filled with every kind of wickedness, evil, greed and depravity. They are full of envy, murder, strife, deceit and malice. They are gossips, slanderers, God-haters, insolent, arrogant and boastful; they invent ways of doing evil; they disobey their parents; they are senseless, faithless, heartless, ruthless. Although they know God's righteous decree that those who do such things deserve death, they not only continue to do these very things but also approve of those who practise them' (Romans 1:24-32).

The classical humanistic dream is for a world without God which is a world full of decent, fair-minded, loving people who together construct a caring and worthwhile society. Paul is saying that that is an illusion, an impossible dream. For, in the words of the Russian novelist Dovstoevsky, 'If God is dead, everything is permissible,' and the sinful heart of man exploits that opportunity to pursue his sin. God gives them up. What Paul writes here in Romans 1 could almost be a commentary on the history of the nineteenth and twentieth centuries in the Western world. In the last century, there emerged a great attack on the Christian understanding of the world. Academics launched themselves with fervour into biblical criticism and made all kinds of accusations (most of which have since been proved to be totally unfounded) against the reliability of the biblical documents. A number of influential scientists proclaimed that Darwinian evolution had 'disproved' God. Writers like G. E. Moore and Lytton Strachey, and playwrights

like G. B. Shaw attacked and derided the Christian
faith, and the impression was given that soon a new and
better world, a freer and fairer world, would emerge.
But now, as we look back we can see that the way society
has gone is rather different. As we perhaps view our own
land, in which murders are up by 50% on the 1960s, and
violence against the person has increased by 5% every
year for the last decade, as we see one in three marriages
ending in divorce and all the loneliness and damage that
does to children – we surely see the same progression
which Paul speaks of in Romans 1. We are seeing something of the disintegration of society. We are seeing
something of the present outworking of the wrath of
God, as God lets people go their own way.

When people reject God, one of the most terrible
aspects of his judgement is that God gives them what
they want – God gives them over to their own ways and
their inevitable fruits.

2. The second aspect of God's wrath is *his eternal
judgement*. The Christian message speaks of heaven,
but it also speaks of hell. There is a coming day of
judgement.

In chapter 2 of his letter to the Romans, the apostle
Paul writes, 'But because of your stubbornness and your
unrepentant heart, you are storing up wrath against
yourself for the day of God's wrath, when his righteous
judgement will be revealed. God "will give to each person according to what he has done". To those who by
persistence in doing good seek glory, honour and
immortality, he will give eternal life. But for those who
are self-seeking and who reject the truth and follow evil,
there will be wrath and anger. There will be trouble and
distress for every human being who does evil . . . but
glory, honour and peace for everyone who does good . . .
For God does not show favouritism' (Romans 2:5-11).

The idea of a coming day of judgement is discounted

by most people today, but in the light of all we have seen
before about God and man and the world, a day of
judgement follows very logically. Indeed, it is true that
without that coming day of judgement we ourselves
would call God unjust. We look at many things which go
on in the present world, we perhaps see the poor
oppressed and children mistreated, we hear of frauds
and swindles and people getting away with it while
others lose out desperately. We say, 'Where is the justice
in the world? If there is a God, why doesn't he do something?' And, indeed, if God never did anything, he
would be guilty of injustice. But there is a coming day of
judgement on which the books of justice will be balanced
and sinners punished.

In the quotation from Romans 2 Paul tells us that the
day of judgement is certainly coming. On that day
everyone will be judged according to how they have
lived. To those who have done nothing but good, God
will give eternal life; to sinners he will bring terrible
trouble and eternal distress. It will all be just and fair.
The only difficulty is, of course, that every single one of
us is a sinner. Not one of us has lived so as constantly to
seek good and do the right. Not one of us can be counted
worthy of eternal life. Not one of us merits acceptance
with God. We are all sinners and we all merit his
condemnation.

This day of judgement, which leads to heaven or hell,
is the most awesome aspect of God's judgement on the
world. And lest we think that this is something which has
just been dreamed up by the apostle Paul, we ought to
realize that *all* the writers of the New Testament refer to
God's judgement. In particular we ought to realize that
Jesus himself is recorded as speaking most plainly and
often on this subject (e.g. Matthew 7:13,14; 10:28;
11:22; 12:42; 13:41-42; 16:26; 18:9; 22:13). It is from the
lips of Jesus that we hear of the lost going away into
eternal punishment (Matthew 25:46).

Here then we see Christianity's diagnosis. Here we see mankind's greatest need.

Man is the pinnacle of creation, with the vast dignity of being made in the image of God. Man is aware of the difference between right and wrong. He is a moral creature accountable to God. But man has rejected God, and has rebelled against God, wishing to put himself in God's place. We daily commit high treason against the throne of the Creator by our self-centred lives. Because of this we are cut off from our Maker and exposed to the just condemnation and judgement of God. That is our lost condition.

But that is not the end of the story. God is not only a holy God; he is also a God of unspeakable love and compassion.

We have seen that Christianity teaches that Jesus is God become man. But why did he come to our world? Why did God enter history? The answer is because of man's lostness. Writing to his young friend Timothy, Paul puts it like this: 'Here is a trustworthy saying that deserves full acceptance: Christ Jesus came into the world to save sinners' (1 Timothy 1:15). Why did God become man? Because although God is angry with sin, yet still he loves us. He came to make a way of salvation. He came in order that all who believe might be rescued. That was his purpose, and that purpose led him to the cross.

We are sinners. We are guilty. Our problem is intrinsically a moral problem. It is with that in mind that we ask our third question about the basic message of Christianity: 'Why did Jesus die on the cross?'

---

*The lawyer and writer John Mortimer, in his autobiography *Clinging to the Wreckage,* interestingly comments concerning Kenneth Tynan that what he calls a 'Puritan conscience' is essential to the true libertine.

†It is interesting that Robert Meister, in the book *A Literary Guide to Seduction,* has remarked that even today every seduction scene is an allegory of the Fall.

References

1. Francis Schaeffer and C. Everett Koop, *Whatever Happened to the Human Race?*, Marshall, Morgan and Scott, 1980, p.84.
2. Francis Schaeffer, *He is there and he is not silent*, Hodder & Stoughton, 1973, p.38.
3. See *The Listener* magazine, 1987.

7.
Good news for everyone

School staff rooms can be stale, smoky, cynical places. But I can remember one lunch-time, while I was working as a teacher, sitting around with a group of colleagues and somehow we started discussing why some of the great sayings of Jesus – sayings like 'I am the light of the world', 'I am the bread of life', or 'I am the good shepherd' – can be so attractive and touch so many chords with us. Even the non-Christians there said that they found in quieter moments that such words spoke to them and touched their hearts.

We came to the conclusion that one of the reasons such words have a magnetism and attraction about them is because *they hold out a sense of hope*. They hold out a sense of the possibility of a better life and a fresh start. Inwardly we think, 'He is the light of the world – I wish I could see where I'm going in life,' or again, we think, 'He gives living water – that's so different from my own failing and rather jaded resources.' Such promises of hope, of a new life, of the slate wiped clean and a fresh beginning, somehow so poignantly touch our deepest needs as human beings.

So far we have seen that Christianity has concluded that we are all sinners before a holy God. Whether we are religious or irreligious, men or women, wise or foolish, rich or poor, reckless or respectable, at bottom we are all compulsive self-centred rebels against God. We are condemned, lost and cut off from the life of God. And in the light of the staff-room discussion, Christianity would say to us, 'You feel your lostness, your hopelessness and emptiness without God. That's why those words of Jesus ring bells with you and speak to your heart. You are lost and alienated from God who made you.'

But the Christian message is not one of gloom and despondency. Having brought us to this very low point, having confronted us with the lostness and hopelessness of mankind, we have more to say – much more! There is good news, there is hope, there is a fresh start and a secure eternal future; God really does offer you a new life and forgiveness and this comes through faith in Jesus Christ. This is how Paul puts it in his letter to the Romans: 'But now a righteousness from God, apart from law, has been made known, to which the Law and the Prophets testify. This righteousness from God comes through faith in Jesus Christ to all who believe. There is no difference, for all have sinned and fall short of the glory of God, and are justified freely by his grace through the redemption that came by Christ Jesus. God presented him as a sacrifice of atonement, through faith in his blood. He did this to demonstrate his justice, because in his forbearance he had left the sins committed beforehand unpunished – he did it to demonstrate his justice at the present time, so as to be just and the one who justifies those who have faith in Jesus' (Romans 3:21-26).

This is a summary of the heart of the gospel. We will look at these verses in some depth. Christianity has got good news. Let's note four things about it.

1. It is a message of faith in Christ

At this turning-point, as he begins to unpack the good

news, it is faith in Christ which is the great thing on Paul's mind. Four times in the space of just five verses he mentions it. *Faith* is the thread that runs through this passage. So before we go any further let us be clear what faith is, because by faith in Christ comes God's forgiveness and new life.

The original New Testament word for faith is defined from the lexicons as *'the trust that a person might put in another person'*. So faith is not just intellectual assent, nor is it the power of positive thinking, but it is personal trust in another person. It is the trust a child might have in his father or mother. It is the trust a person might have in a very close and reliable friend. It is the trust a wife might put in her husband. Faith is believing God.

Do you know the Old Testament story of David and Jonathan? They were the greatest of friends, and Jonathan was King Saul's son. But King Saul had become very jealous of David because he was aware that God had chosen David to become the next king after him. Saul became so jealous that he began to seek David to kill him. David went into hiding, and only Jonathan knew where he was. Jonathan could easily have betrayed David to his father. But David trusted Jonathan not to betray him, and Jonathan did not, because he knew what was right and he was a good friend to David. David trusted Jonathan with his life. That is a picture of faith.

Or here is another illustration of faith, this time from secular history. It concerns Alexander the Great, the all-conquering Greek soldier of the ancient world. During one of his early military campaigns against the Persians under King Darius, Alexander was taken ill with a fever. Just as his doctor Philippus was handing him a glass of medicine, he received a letter telling him that Philippus had been bribed by Darius to poison him. Alexander knew and trusted Philippus as a great friend, and to show his trust he handed him the letter to read as he drank the medicine. Of course, Alexander soon recovered from the fever.

The thread running through the verses in Romans 3 is this. Just as David trusted his friend Jonathan, just as Alexander trusted his physician, so you and I must trust Jesus Christ, the friend and physician of sinners. By that personal trust in the person of Jesus, we will know God's forgiveness and new life. Faith in Christ is the essence of Christianity and that is what Paul is quick to urge upon us.

Now in the rest of his explanation of Christianity, which he gives in his letter to the Romans, Paul has a great deal to say about the full meaning of what it is to become a Christian. He will go on to talk about how the hold of sin on us can be broken and we can begin to live a life of love and service towards God and men. He is going to speak about how it is that the Christian is someone who receives the power of God's Holy Spirit and that he takes away spiritual blindness and enables the Christian to make progress against sin and to live differently. He is going to speak about the Christian's experience of the love of God, and the peace which Christ brings, and heaven which awaits the Christian, and many other things. Paul obviously can't say everything at once. So he begins at the foundation. It is plain that our most fundamental need before God is a moral need. It is once this is dealt with that the rest follows. The beginning of this good news concerns how God has provided for that need. It is about how God has provided a 'righteousness' for sinners. It is about how God has met that moral need in the most profound way. It is about how God can put people right in the light of his holy law.

2. The gift of righteousness

'But now a righteousness from God, apart from law, has been made known, to which the Law and the Prophets testify' (Romans 3:21).

Why is man cut off from God? Why is man under God's condemnation? Why don't people know the life of God in their hearts? The root of it all is because they are guilty before God. We have broken God's law. We are selfish and ungodly. We are unrighteous. That is the root of it. We have sinned and we stand before God the Judge, in God's courtroom, guilty. We are all wrong in the sight of his law, and these other things – the fact that God seems so far away, and that we know no lasting peace or joy – are just the consequences of this guilt.

So if we are to know God and the new life he offers, this guilt, this matter of having sinned and broken God's law is the first thing that must be put right.

The beginning of Paul's good news is that 'now', because Jesus Christ has come, now, even though you and I are sinners, we can have our guilt taken away and have righteousness, right standing in the eyes of God: 'But now a righteousness from God . . . has been made known.'

Paul tells us three things about this righteousness.

It is 'apart from the law'
'But now a righteousness from God, *apart from law*, has been made known, to which the Law and the Prophets testify.' It is 'apart from the law'. In other words, this being clear before the judgement bar of God does not come by our trying to keep God's law. It couldn't. Even if we could keep God's law perfectly from now on, that would never make up for our past failures. And then we

have these wretched deceitful hearts of ours, so that even if we could keep the law outwardly, we could never keep it inwardly. The good news is that this righteousness is precisely suited to sinners, because it does not arise from us or our own efforts with respect to God's law. Although the Old Testament – the Law and the Prophets – speaks about this righteousness, it does not become ours by law-keeping. It is 'apart from the law'.

It is a gift from God to all who believe
This righteousness is *not* something of our own doing; rather it is a gift. 'This righteousness from God *comes through* faith in Jesus Christ to all who believe.' It comes to us. It is a present, a gift freely given, to be received by faith in Christ. The wonderful truth is that God is giving away acquittal notices for judgement day. The words 'clear of the charge', 'not guilty', 'righteous' are being written now in the books of heaven against the names of everyone who has personal faith in Jesus Christ. This righteousness, this status of being right in the sight of God, is a gift to be received by faith.

It is offered to us all
'There is no difference, for all have sinned and fall short of the glory of God, and are justified freely by his grace . . .' No one is excluded. This is an offer not just for one particular nationality or class of people. Nor is it just for nice people. It is offered freely to all, because we are all equal, we have all sinned, we all have the same need. God offers this gift of righteousness to us all and says, 'If you trust my Son, Jesus Christ – it's yours.'

So Paul tells us of this marvellous gift of righteousness. But then we may well have a question: 'How can God do that? How can he just give a free pardon to us? How can he declare people righteous who have been patently unrighteous, lawbreakers and sinners?' The

answer is in the next matter which Paul mentions in these
verses.

3. The death of Christ

It is the death of Jesus on the cross at Calvary which
enables God to give people the gift of righteousness.

Now this gift of righteousness by God has a special
name in the New Testament. It is called 'justification',
and a person who has received the gift of righteous status
before God's law is said to be 'justified'. The word justification is from a court of law. It is the opposite of condemnation. When a judge pronounces a defendant guilty,
that is condemnation. When the judge pronounces a person innocent, that is justification. It is a legal declaration. It does not change the person. The defendant is
still the same man after the judge's declaration as he was
before. But it changes the man's *status* in the eyes of the
law. He is now known as an innocent and free man.

God is able to do that for sinners because of the death
of Jesus and we will understand how if we understand
two key words in what Paul next says. We are 'justified
freely by his grace through the *redemption* that came by
Christ Jesus. God presented him as a *sacrifice of atonement* [or *propitiation*], through faith in his blood.' The
two expressions we need to understand related to
Christ's cross are 'redemption' and 'propitiation', or
'sacrifice of atonement'.

What Jesus did for sinners in dying on the cross is
termed 'redemption'. What is that? It is a word which
comes from the slave market. A person has fallen into
slavery and is now owned by a master and stands in the
slave market. But now a friend comes along and pays a
price to the master and *the slave is set free*. When that
happened he is said to have been 'redeemed', a price was
paid which set him free. In the Old Testament the

prophet Hosea did this for his loose-living wife Gomer. She was a prostitute and the downward spiral of her life ended her up in the slave market. But Hosea still loved her, just as God loves sinners, and he went and paid the price for her and took her home to himself. She had been saved from slavery. She had been redeemed.

But what happened at the cross? Well, we are all sinners. We were justly owned by God's law. We had broken God's commands, we had turned from him to serve sin and self, and God's law had just claims upon us that we should face the consequences of our sin and be punished, consigned to hell at the coming judgement. But Christ came and died on the cross and in doing so he paid the penalty our sins deserve, he met our debt of sin with his own blood. The demands of justice have no more claims on us, for out of pure love and grace Christ has *redeemed* all who believe.

The second expression used in connection with Christ's death is 'propitiation' or 'sacrifice of atonement'. What does that mean? Well, not only was there a legal side to our sin, but there was also a personal side. Not only was God's law broken, but God was angry with our sin, just as I was angry when one of my children was attacked. 'Propitiation' has to do with the wrath and anger of God towards our sin. By his death on the cross Christ not only satisfied the demands of God's law; he also quenched the wrath of God towards us, he pacified the anger of God towards us because of our sin, so that God is now able to receive us and accept us.

Now it is worth noting that, as Paul explains it, it is not simply a loving Jesus pacifying an angry God the Father. That is too simplistic. Notice that Paul makes it clear that the Father 'presented' Christ as a sacrifice of atonement or propitiation. In other words God sent Jesus with the purpose of pacifying himself. It was not that the Father was all anger and Jesus was all love. No, in his anger God loved us – just as any father who sees his children go wrong is both angry and loving towards them. And in his love God the Father asked God the Son to come and die for us that we might be forgiven, and Jesus agreed to do that.

All these three things, justification, redemption and propitiation, can helpfully be seen as fitting together in what is sometimes called 'the Salvation Triangle'. It gives us an overview of what God in his love has done for sinners at the cross.

God justifies Christians – all those who have personal faith in Christ. He can do that because, dying in our place, Jesus has both pacified God's wrath (propitiation), and by his death has met the righteous demands of God's law which we had broken (redemption), so that we are now right with God.[1]

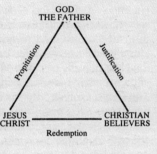

But some people, viewing this plan of salvation, say, 'Why did God have to do all that in order that we might be saved? Why couldn't God just let us off? Why couldn't God just forget about sin and accept us?' Paul deals with that in the final verses of this section of Romans that we are considering.

4. The justice of God

God could not just let people off and sweep sin under the carpet and forget about it. If he did that God would basically be saying that sin doesn't matter. He would in effect then be saying that the difference between right and wrong doesn't matter, and that would make him no better than the devil. God cannot be like that. He is righteous, just and holy. He wanted, in his love and kindness, to save us, but it had to be accomplished in a way which did not compromise his commitment to right instead of wrong. This had to be done not just to others' satisfaction, but to his own satisfaction. God needed to work out our salvation in a way which he knew to be right and just.

Now, according to Paul, the death of Christ satisfied God's justice in two ways.

The continuation of world history

Of Christ's cross, Paul writes, 'He did this to demonstrate his justice, because in his forbearance he had left the sins committed beforehand unpunished . . .' You see, there is a sense in which as soon as sin entered the world God should have destroyed the world. After all, if we see something that is evil and we have the power to put a stop to it but fail to do anything about it, we could rightly be accused of wrongdoing. It is not right to sit back, as it were, and let something evil grow and continue when we could stop it. God could have stopped sin and evil right at the beginning, by destroying the world and everything in it as soon as sin entered. But God, in his forbearance and love, did not want to do that. He wanted world history to be lived out, so that he would not be thwarted by evil and, as they appeared on the stage of world history, he could save his people. What Paul is telling us here is that the death of Christ sets the record straight for the fact that God has left the world unpunished and allowed its continuation for so long. In this sense it is true that every man, woman and child who has ever lived or who ever will live owes their whole existence and every enjoyment that they may have in life to the death of Jesus Christ.

2. Eternal salvation for all who believe

But the primary focus of the death of Christ is concerned

with judgement day. It was that all who believe might justly be forgiven their sins and find eternal acceptance with God. Paul therefore goes on in what he is writing about the cross and says, 'He did it to demonstrate his justice at the present time, so as to be just and the one who justifies the man who believes in Jesus Christ.'

No one can point the finger at God and say that his free gift of forgiveness and salvation is unjust. The death of Christ for all who believe secures that fact. In the road where I live there are severe parking restrictions. Sometimes people overstay their time and receive a fixed penalty fine which the traffic warden sticks to the windscreen of the offending car. The penalty must be paid. But let us suppose a friend comes down the road and recognizes a car with a fine ticket on. Let us suppose that he decides to take that ticket and write a cheque and pay the fine. Then, even though the offending driver hasn't paid, nevertheless the fine, the penalty, has been paid, and the county court cannot ask for it to be paid again. Justice has been done and the offender has gone free, and it is all perfectly just. Grace and kindness have set the offender free. That is just a small illustration of the profound act of friendship and love which Jesus Christ has performed for sinners at the cross. Our sins deserved eternal condemnation. It was a huge debt. But because of who Jesus was, not just a man but God incarnate, when he died on the cross he was well able to pay the debt of our sins. Indeed the death of Christ is worth so much that it is more than sufficient to cover all our sins and the sins of all who will trust themselves to him. It saves them from hell and it secures them for heaven. And as God looks at the balances of justice he is well satisfied that the death of his Son on our behalf enables him 'to be just, and the justifier of the man who has faith in Jesus'. Which brings us back again to where we started this section, the need for personal trust in the Lord Jesus

Christ, that the new life and forgiveness which God offers might be ours.

'Who is Jesus Christ?', 'What is man?', 'Why the cross?' As we have tried to answer those three questions from the New Testament and especially from Paul's letter to the Romans, we have seen something of the principal components of the Christian faith. We have seen that the life of Jesus is the most remarkable life in history. Christians believe that Jesus is none other than God become man. Our Maker has walked the earth and called us to follow him. To ignore his call to faith is to walk into eternal darkness.

We have tried to show that when we ask the question 'What is man?', the only answer which really makes sense of man is the Christian answer. We are the apex of God's creation, made in the image of God, and made for friendship with God. But we have rebelled against God. We have not wanted him to be our Lord and Master. Because of man's rebellion as the head of creation, all creation has fallen under the condemnation of God and is out of touch with the Creator. This is the reason for the sorry state of the world. Christ has come and called us to follow him, and for us not to do that simply confirms Christianity's view of us as rebels against God.

We have also seen the marvellous central reason why Jesus came. He came to die, in order that he might pay for our sins, and so God and man might be reconciled. The cross is God's great display of love and grace towards us. By the cross he has done everything necessary for all who will believe to be reconciled to him. As far as God is concerned, through the cross there are absolutely no barriers to any of us coming to him and finding forgiveness and new life. If there are any barriers they are barriers of our own making, not God's. In the light of the cross the apostle Paul can call us to faith and say, 'We implore you on Christ's behalf: Be reconciled to God.'

This is the crux of the Christian message. This is the explanation of our world and our situation which alone makes sense of everything. But much more, this is the good news for everyone.

References

1.   James M. Boice, *Foundations of Christian Faith*, IVP 1986, p.323.

8.
Suffering – the final objection

Suffering occurs in our world on a heartbreaking and gigantic scale. Very often the size of the world's tragedy is hidden from us. The undertakers are discreet. Most of us only observe the suffering of the poorer parts of the world from the safe distance of a TV camera and a communications satellite.

But the scale of suffering in our world is horrifying. Here is one statistic, for example, which may just help us to begin to comprehend the proportions of the problem. In the twelve months of 1986 fifteen million infants and children died, mostly in the poorer countries of the world. That is equivalent to 100 jumbo jet crashes with no survivors every day of the year. For every minute spent reading this book, twenty-six babies in the world have died.

For many people, the greatest objection to Christianity is, understandably, the problem of suffering. They say that Christianity may make a lot of sense up to a point, but if there is a loving God how can he possibly allow the suffering, pain and evil which we see in the world? When we are confronted with tragedy and anguish, particularly when it seems so senseless, without rhyme or reason, the very common reaction is to get angry with God, and bitterly to reject God.

It may well have been in this frame of mind that some

people confronted Jesus himself with the problem of suffering. We read about it in Luke's Gospel: 'Now there were some present at that time who told Jesus about the Galileans whose blood Pilate had mixed with their sacrifices. Jesus answered, "Do you think that these Galileans were worse sinners than all the other Galileans because they suffered in this way? I tell you, no! But unless you repent, you too will all perish. Or those eighteen who died when the tower in Siloam fell on them – do you think they were more guilty than all the others living in Jerusalem? I tell you, no! But unless you repent, you too will all perish"' (Luke 13: 1-5).

Here people come and confront Jesus with something in the news. The Roman governor Pilate had brutally dealt to death some folk from Jesus' home region of Galilee, perhaps because they were protesting about the injustices of Roman oppression in Palestine. These people were seemingly in the middle of offering sacrifices to God, yet God allowed this to happen. It was all so unjust. And Jesus goes on to widen the debate, by speaking of an industrial accident in which eighteen ordinary people had been killed outright when a tower collapsed. Why did God allow that?

There are no slick and comfortable answers to the problem of suffering. But let us think about the problem to begin with by trying to grasp something of Jesus' reply. Does Christianity have anything helpful and worthwhile to say about this terrible subject of suffering? For us all one day it will no longer be a subject which we can treat academically. Suffering, some time or other, will touch our own lives. We all have to face death. What does Christianity have to say in answer to someone who says, 'I can't believe in God because of all the suffering'? He does not give a comfortable answer, but Jesus' reply to the people who brought him news of Pilate's brutality is worth considering in some depth.

Rejecting God?

The first thing which is quite striking is that when Jesus is confronted by this tragic news he does not quickly jump to reject God or to explain that God is not ultimately in control. Neither is he so threatened by the question that he feels he must go into a long and detailed defence of the existence of God, or of the fact that God really does care about human beings. Why is that? Why doesn't he feel threatened or stumped?

Here perhaps are three reasons – three things to bear in mind before we quickly jump to reject God because of human suffering.

1.   The argument for rejecting God on the grounds of his supposed injustice because of suffering in the world is logically faulty. C.S. Lewis, before he became a Christian, had to think the problem through. 'My argument against God was that the universe seemed so cruel and unjust,' he says with reference to the atheistic period of his life. 'But how had I got this idea of *just* and *unjust*? A man doesn't call a line crooked unless he has some idea of a straight line. What was I comparing this universe with when I called it unjust? If the whole show was bad and senseless from A to Z, so to speak, why did I, who was supposed to be part of the show, find myself in such violent reaction against it? A man feels wet when he falls into water because man isn't a water animal; a fish wouldn't feel wet. Of course I could have given up my idea of justice by saying that it was nothing but a private idea of my own. But if I did that then my argument against God collapsed too – for the argument depended on saying that the world was really unjust; not that it just didn't happen to please my private fancies. Thus in the very act of trying to prove that God didn't exist – in other words, that the whole of reality was senseless – I found I was forced to assume that one part of reality – namely

my idea of justice – was full of sense. Consequently, atheism turns out to be too simple. If the whole universe has no meaning, we should never have found out that it has no meaning; just as if there were no light in the universe and therefore no creatures with eyes we should never have known it was dark. Dark would be a word without meaning.'[1]

Lewis's argument is the same as that which we considered before in chapter 2, for God's existence. If there is no God, there is no absolute right or wrong, so injustice is meaningless. To accuse God of real injustice is to accept that he is there. Only if God exists do you have a basis on which to charge anyone or anything with being unjust and unfair. So to reject the existence of God on the basis of suffering and injustice is illogical.

Lord Hailsham has made the same point in a slightly different way in his autobiography. He writes, 'You do not get out of your philosophical troubles arising out of the fact of evil by rejecting God. For, as I have tried to point out before, the real problem is not the problem of evil, but the problem of good, not the problem of cruelty and selfishness but the problem of kindness and generosity, not the problem of ugliness but the problem of beauty. If the world is really the hopeless and meaningless jumble which one has to believe it to be if once we reject our value judgements as nothing more than emotional noises, with nothing more in the way of objective truth than a certain biological survival value for the species rather than the individual, evil then presents no difficulty because it does not exist. We must expect to be knocked about a bit in a world which consists only of atoms, molecules and strange particles. But how, then, does it come about that we go through life on assumptions which are perfectly contrary to the facts, that we love our wives and families, thrill with pleasure at the sight of a little bird discreetly dressed in green and black and white, that we rage at injustice inflicted on innocent victims, honour our martyrs, reward our heroes, and even occasionally with difficulty forgive our enemies and do good to those who persecute us and despitefully use us? No, it is light which is the problem, not darkness. It is seeing, not blindness . . . It is love, not callousness. The thing we have to explain in the world is the positive, not the negative. It is this which led me to God in the first place. It is this which leads me to think that I know something about his activity in the world through the Christ of history.'

2.   Rejecting God is not only logically inconsistent, but just from the point of view of pragmatism, it does not leave us any better off. Confronted by the troubles and tragedies of life the old Greek philosophers were able to come up with just three answers. First, there were the cynics. Their idea was that life is painful and meaningless, so just hit out at it. But what good does that do? It just produces joyless, bitter, cynical people! Second, there were the Stoics. In the face of suffering they said you have just got to grin and bear it. Again, that gets us no further forward; we know we have to bear it. Third, there were the Epicureans, whose motto was 'Eat, drink and be merry, for tomorrow we die!' This is just pure escapism and refusal to face reality. The basic thing to see is that none of these approaches to suffering offers any real hope, because to reject God is ultimately to exclude any hope for the suffering and dying world. In God there is hope for those experiencing tragedy. Pragmatically, what is the point of rejecting hope?

3.   The third reason why, perhaps, Jesus did not feel threatened by this question about suffering is because people often reject God over suffering because they have a grave misconception of God. They have an idea of God seated up in his perfect Platonic paradise of heaven, aloof, distant, unmoved, detached from it all – all too ready to judge the world for its misdemeanours, while the world cries out wracked with pain. But that is

not a true picture at all of the God of the Bible. After all, who is the God of the Christian faith? Who is it that these people in Luke 13 have come to ask about suffering? It is Jesus Christ who came to *suffer*, Jesus the suffering Servant.

This prose piece, entitled *The Long Silence,* points out this grand misunderstanding of God in quite an acute way.

'At the end of time, billions of people were scattered on a great plain before God's throne.
Most shrank back from the brilliant light before them. But some groups near the front talked heatedly – not with cringing shame, but with belligerence.

'"Can God judge us? How can he know about suffering?" snapped a pert young brunette. She ripped open a sleeve to reveal a tattooed number from a Nazi concentration camp. "We endured terror. . . beatings. . . torture. . . death!"

'In another group a Negro boy lowered his collar. "What about this?" he demanded, showing an ugly rope burn. "Lynched for no crime but being black!"

'In another crowd, a pregnant schoolgirl with sullen eyes. "Why should I suffer?" she murmured, "It wasn't my fault." Far out across the plain were hundreds of such groups. Each had a complaint against God for the evil and suffering he permitted in his world.
'How lucky God was to live in heaven where all was sweetness and light, where there was no weeping or fear, no hunger or hatred! What did God know of all that man had been forced to endure in this world? For God leads a pretty sheltered life, they said.

'So each of these groups sent forth their leader, chosen

because he had suffered the most. A Jew, a Negro, a person from Hiroshima, a horribly deformed arthritic, a thalidomide child.

'In the centre of the plain they consulted with each other. At last they were ready to present their case. It was rather clever.

'Before God could be qualified to be their judge, he must endure what they had endured. Their decision was that God should be sentenced to life on earth – as a man!

'Let him be born a Jew. Let the legitimacy of his birth be doubted. Give him a work so difficult that even his family will think him out of his mind when he tries to do it. Let him be betrayed by his closest friends. Let him face false charges, be tried by a prejudiced jury and convicted by a cowardly judge. Let him be tortured.

'At last let him see what it means to be terribly alone. Then let him die. Let him die so that there can be no doubt he died. Let there be a great host of witnesses to verify it.

'As each leader announced his portion of the sentence, loud murmurings of approval went up from the throng of people assembled.

'When the last had finished pronouncing sentence there was a long silence. No one uttered a word. No one moved. For all suddenly knew that God had already served his sentence.'[2]

Now obviously man cannot really sit in judgement on God in this way; but you see the point. God is not the comfortable, detached, faraway God – he is Jesus. He himself has been involved in the very depths of tragedy. He has experienced suffering to the utmost. More

than anyone else he understands and sympathizes with
suffering.

So it should not surprise us that when confronted with
this problem of suffering, Jesus does not agree with
those who reject God on this basis. Neither does he get
very defensive about the question. To write God off over
this matter of suffering is far too simple. To do so is illogical; it may give vent to understandable anger but it
brings no answers; and it is often built upon an inaccu-
rate understanding of God.

Suffering and sin

The next point to notice in Jesus' reply is what Jesus does
and does not say about the relationship between suffering and God's judgement because of sin. He accepts that
there is a general relationship between sin and suffering,
but he totally rejects the idea that a conclusion about
personal sin can be drawn from the degree of personal
suffering. Jesus was well aware that sometimes the innocent suffer.

Let us look at these points.

1.   Jesus accepts that suffering is related to sin in a
general way. He says to his hearers, 'Unless you repent,
you too will perish.' The acceptance that mankind is
under God's judgement because of sin is fundamental to
Jesus' answer here. Sin, not God, has brought about the
terrible state of affairs in the world. If there was no sin
there would be no suffering. God had originally made a
perfect world. But when man sinfully turned away from
God, suffering entered to mar God's wonderful creation. Suffering was never part of God's original plan.
Thus, Jesus went around doing good, alleviating suffering and pain wherever he could. These things are not
what God desires for mankind. Suffering is in the world

because the world has, by its sin, put itself under God's judgement.

It is in that context that Jesus points out that the Galileans whom Pilate had killed must not be thought of as being singled out for such a horrible death because they were worse sinners than others. He calls on his hearers to repent before it is too late, otherwise they too will all perish. Without salvation we are all on our way to hell. Plainly Jesus sees these folk as sinners in need of repentance. As elsewhere, he takes universal sinfulness as basic. And sinfulness exposes us all to God's judgement.

What Jesus is actually implying here is tremendously important for an understanding of what the Bible says about suffering. What Jesus is implying is this: when we ask the question. 'Why did that person suffer?' or 'How come that happened to him or her?' we are really asking the wrong question. In the light of the fact that sin quite properly exposes people to God's judgement, the question we ought to be asking is 'Why don't we all suffer more than we do? Why aren't we all in hell already?' This is the implication of what Jesus is saying and it is a very sobering thought. Jesus would make us realize that given the situation of the world in sin, the fact that health and strength are the norm for so many people is the remarkable thing. The fact that given mankind's rebellion against God, God still continues to supply more than enough food for the world to go round – if only we would share it – that is the remarkable thing. The fact that a holy God continues to give us life and breath even though we are sinners, that is the marvellous anachronism.

This approach of Jesus throws a completely different light on the problem of suffering.

2. But secondly, in this consideration of suffering. Jesus declares that there is generally speaking no one-to-

one correspondence between sin and suffering in this life. The whole human race is now exposed to suffering, but there is no way in which we can make deductions about a person's individual sin by observing his or her individual suffering.

The story of Job, for example, in the Old Testament, makes the acceptance of such a tit-for-tat theology of suffering impossible. Suffering of every possible kind invades Job's life. His wealth is stolen. His business collapses. His children die. He personally is inflicted with the most acute and painful skin disease. Then his friends immediately jump to the conclusion that Job must have committed some great and secret sin for this to have happened to him, so they continually counsel him to own up and confess his sin. But Job is not a great sinner. On God's own declaration at the beginning of the story, Job is the most holy man on earth. So why is he suffering, then? It is part of an attack by Satan on the character of God. Satan is saying that God is so worthless that people only serve him for what they can get out of him and if God allows trouble to come into the life of his friend Job, then Job will walk out on God and curse him. But Satan is defeated, because although Job understandably gets very impatient in the midst of his trial and agony, he refuses to curse God. He still loves God even though he does not know why this suffering has come upon him. Job then, is the great counter-example of the idea that there is a one-to-one relationship between sin and suffering.

In fact the occurrence of suffering is even more 'random' than the story of Job would show us. Once in Jesus' ministry he came across a man who had been born blind and his disciples ask, 'Who sinned, this man or his parents, that he was born blind?' (John 9:2). Jesus' reply was that this man's blindness was not the direct result of anyone's sin; then, in order to display the power and glory of God, Jesus went on to heal him.

Although there is no direct correspondence which we can deduce between individual sin and individual suffering, the general relationship between sin and suffering does in a way explain the frequent 'randomness' and senselessness of suffering. How? Why? Well, what is sin? The Bible defines it as *lawlessness* (1 John 3:4). First of all, of course, it is rejection of God's moral laws. But it goes further than that. At bottom sin is a rejection of and rebellion against all God's ways. It should not surprise us when we realize that sin often breaks not only moral laws, but even the laws of logic and reason. It is born out of the womb of satanic chaos. How many people will continue in a particular sin, even when it is sapping their health? How many go on in sin even when it threatens their job or their family? Sin is unreasonable.[3] And if sin is at root senseless, irrational and absurd, it should not surprise us that suffering, the great concomitant of sin, the great consequence of sin entering the world, is also often senseless and heartbreakingly unjust.

The tragedy is that when mankind rejected God and chose sin, we were placing ourselves under the judgement of God, and part of that judgement was that God gave us up to what we had chosen, the unjust and the ultimately irrational. In choosing the way of sin, man was handing himself over into the hands of destructive and irrational forces. So suffering often appears totally unjust. It is terribly misguided of us to try to draw some conclusion about an individual's sin from his or her suffering. We are not to judge others. Only God is the judge of us all. But sin and suffering are inextricable allies.

3. However, there is a third element in Jesus' reply which must not be missed. Twice, as he answers the people who came to tell him the news of the suffering and death of the Galileans, Jesus says, 'But unless you repent, you too will perish!' We have noted already that Jesus sees mankind as already exposed to judgement,

suffering and condemnation to hell, but he also speaks here of the need of repentance and the benefit which repentance brings.

It may be that Jesus was simply underlining the unexpected way in which these folk died and is therefore urging people to repent while there is time. I am sure that is true. But there seems to be more to what Jesus is saying. After all, what is the point of repentance? 'Unless you repent, you too will all perish.' The implication is that 'If you do repent then you will not perish.' Jesus is indicating that repentance, turning from sin and turning to God, leads in some sense to escape from death and suffering.

What was Jesus talking about?

The kingdom of God

Christianity has always taken seriously the idea that history is leading somewhere. It has always proclaimed that history is building up to a climax when this old world with all its sin and suffering will be done away and the universe will be transformed. This is how the apostle Paul looks to the future as he contemplates the difficulties of his life. 'I consider that our present sufferings are not worth comparing with the glory that will be revealed in us. The creation waits in eager expectation for the sons of God to be revealed. For the creation was subjected to frustration, not by its own choice, but by the will of the one who subjected it, in hope that the creation itself will be liberated from its bondage and brought into the glorious freedom of the children of God.' Of course, this expectation for the future has its roots in the Old Testament. The life of Israel was often troubled, and at such times God would remind his ancient people of his promise to send the Messiah who would herald a new age. The prophet Isaiah, for example, speaks in idyllic terms of God's King coming to reign, bringing in peace and righteousness (e.g. Isaiah 9:6,7; 11:1-9). Indeed the apostle Peter borrows Isaiah's language to speak to suffering Christians and remind them that we eagerly 'look forward to a new heaven and a new earth, the home of righteousness' (2 Peter 3:13). It is this future expectation of the kingdom of God, scorned by Karl Marx and modern sceptics, which has always stood as Christianity's final answer to the problem of suffering.

It would seem that at the back of Jesus' mind, as he was warning people of their need of repentance, he knew that repentance and trust in himself were the means by which his hearers could be rescued from this world of suffering and enter the kingdom of God. In Christ, God is seeking to save men and women from this world, where they are under the dominion of sin and suffering, and to deliver them totally into the amazing blessings of his kingdom.

But can we take this seriously? Can God actually wrap up this old universe and bring in a new one?

Surely, the very straightforward answer to this is simply that if we believe that God created this world, this universe, then what is to stop him creating another one? This old world which has been devastated and tragically degraded by sin and its effects surely can be replaced.

This becomes even clearer when we recognize once again what was pointed out in chapter 2. We saw there that the Bible's teaching concerning the relationship between God and the world is such that God continually sustains the world. He is not a watchmaker, who set the clockwork of the universe going and then having wound it up went away and left it. The universe is not self-sustaining. Rather every moment of every day all things are upheld by God's power.

There is a helpful illustration of a TV picture which enables us to understand something of God's continual activity of sustaining the world. The Bible's teaching is that the world is like the picture we see on the screen of a TV set. The picture is there and it looks as if it is a little self-sustained world, going on its own. You can see cause and effect between everything that is going on in the picture. But, of course, all the time the picture is sustained by the electron gun at the back of the TV tube and if that is cut off the whole of the picture collapses.

That is how the world is according to the Bible. We think it is self-sustaining, like the superficial appearance of the TV picture. But in fact, all the time it is totally dependent upon the upholding power and sustaining command of God. The New Testament book of Hebrews speaks of Christ in just this way: 'The Son is the radiance of God's glory and the exact representation of his being, sustaining all things by his powerful word' (Hebrews 1:3).

Scientists say, quite rightly, that the universe runs according to various laws of physics. That is fine. But where did those laws come from? And what makes them always the same, never changing in order that the world might run? It is God's power and God's command.

So to bring the present world to an end, all God would have to do is to cease upholding this world, to cease the sustaining work he has been doing since creation. And to create a new world, God would simply have to create again as he did at the beginning. It would be no more difficult for God to create a new world than it is for you and me to change channels on a TV set! A new heavens and a new earth are well within God's capabilities.

In fact what God will do, according to the Scripture, at the end of time, is not to send this world into oblivion and start again from scratch. Rather he will take the present world and transform it. There is a continuity between this present world and the world to come. The end of this world is a judgement day in which all evil will be put down and the present world totally cleansed, restructured and renewed. The dead will be raised and

God's people of history will become part of eternity. God does not discard this world into the wastebin of nothingness, but rather he will cleanse and totally transform it into a new heavens and new earth, and those who have suffered in this life will enter a world where there is no more suffering, no more tears, no more pain, no more death. They will enter the kingdom of God in all its fulness.

And God has not left the matter of his coming kingdom in the realm of mere speculation. He has actually given a demonstration of its reality. In our own history he has given a preview of it in Jesus Christ.

Jesus died on the cross to deal with sin. But God raised him from the dead never to die again. This matter of a new world of eternal life, free from sin and pain and death, is no idle tale. Christ's resurrection from the dead displays God's ability to raise the dead and to bestow everlasting life upon human beings.

This is why the New Testament speaks of the resurrection of Jesus in terms of 'firstfruits' (1 Corinthians 15:23) and of Jesus as 'the firstborn from among the dead' (Colossians 1:18). The firstfruits of the harvest had a special significance for the Old Testament Jew, and it is against the background of the Old Testament that the New is written. The firstfruits of the harvest were the fruit which ripened in advance of the rest of the harvest. It was an early example of what the rest of the harvest would be like and pointed to the fact that the rest of the harvest was on its way. Again, the firstborn child of a family was of particular significance. Not only would a firstborn son later become the head of the family, but of course, the arrival of the firstborn showed that the couple were fruitful and that therefore more children were possible. In just the same way as the firstfruits point to the rest of the harvest and the firstborn to the rest of the family, so the resurrection of Jesus points to the general resurrection at the end of time. Ultimately it

points to the reality of the new world that God has promised and the kingdom of eternal life for all who belong to
him.

Jesus took the problem of suffering seriously. He
often healed the afflicted during his earthly ministry.
But that could only give temporary relief. One day, even
those people had to face death. Jesus came to do something far more permanent concerning the problem of
suffering. He came to suffer himself. As he, who was
God in the flesh, suffered on the cross, suffering was in
a way reversed. As Jesus suffered, sin and suffering were
conquered. As Jesus hung upon the cross, sin and suffering found that they had, as it were, bitten off more than
they could chew. The door to eternal life was forced
open for all who will come. He came and died for our
sins that all who believe in him might have everlasting
life. He rose from the dead to show that the life he offers
is a wonderful reality.

References

1.   Quoted by P. E. Hughes, *Hope for a Despairing World*,
Eerdmanns.
2.   Quoted by Stephen Travis, *The Jesus Hope*, IVP.
3.   Donald Macleod, *Banner of Truth* magazine, no. 70-71,
p.16.

9.
Becoming a Christian

This book began by facing the suggestion that the Christian faith is a confidence trick, a spectacular deception akin to, but far more serious than, the story of the king's new suit of clothes. The approach we have taken has therefore concentrated on trying to set out something of the reasons for believing the Christian faith to be true. We have seen that the popular idea that Christianity is just psychological, a mixture of sentiment and wishful thinking, does not bear close scrutiny. This led us on to consider some of the positive reasons for, and the logic behind, belief in the God of the Bible. We argued that, for all the many philosophies and ideologies which abound, in fact only the assumptions which Christianity makes about God and the world make sense of reality. Next we tried to sift some of the historical evidence which relates to the person of the Lord Jesus Christ. Then we looked at some of the most fundamental tenets of the Christian gospel, basing our investigation on the three questions: 'Who is Jesus Christ?' 'What is man?' and 'Why did Jesus die on the cross?' We saw there an assessment of mankind and mankind's needs which is strikingly different from many of today's ideas, but which seems to make a great deal of sense. Lastly we have looked at something of Christianity's wonderful answer to the desperate problem of suffering.

But Christian faith, although we have tried to approach it intellectually, is not to be seen simply in terms of intellectual assent. An acceptance of Christian truths with the mind is a necessary part of Christian faith, but on its own falls short of what God calls us to do in response to his Son Jesus. If you have found, as you have read this book, that Christianity makes sense, then you must take it further. You must come to personal faith and trust in the Lord Jesus.

We have seen before that by 'faith in Christ' the New Testament is talking about the kind of total trust one person would put in another. We must come to such personal faith in the Lord Jesus Christ if we are truly to be Christians and know the salvation and new life Christ brings.

One of the Bible's pictures of the relationship between Christ and those who believe is that of a husband and a bride. Christ is the Husband, we are the bride. We can read all the books on Christianity and go to church a million times, but until we have personal faith in Christ we will have nothing and find nothing. Faith in Christ is very like the faith that a bride puts in her husband on her wedding day. She gives herself wholly into his care, protection, service and love, for life. This is what we must do if we would come to Christ. Such total commitment to Christ is the only thing that is fitting because of who he is. He is God our Maker. He is God the Saviour.

In the light of the biblical picture of Christ the Husband and of us as his bride, some people have found it helpful to take the words of the old marriage service and think them through in terms of trusting Christ.

What is it to come to Christ? Ask yourself these questions: 'Will you have Jesus Christ to be your Saviour? Will you live for him? Will you be subject to him, serve him, love, honour and keep him whether you are in sickness or in health and forsaking your sin and all other gods keep only to him so long as you shall live?'

Can you answer those questions with a sincere affirmative? Then can you pray the following? 'I ....take you, Jesus Christ, to be my Lord and Saviour, to have and to hold from this day forward, for better for worse, for richer for poorer, in sickness and in health, to love, cherish and to obey, till death comes and then for evermore, according to God's holy gospel, and thereto I give you my promise.'

As you approach the Lord in such a way, and as the Holy Spirit works in your heart, you will become a Christian, a true child of God. Your sins will be forgiven. You will come to know the Lord. Jesus has promised: 'All that the Father gives me will come to me, and whoever comes to me I will never drive away' (John 6:37).